Read by Zed in

The Year of Finding Memory

THE YEAR
OF FINDING MEMORY

A Memoir

JUDY FONG BATES

Random House Canada

www.randomhouse.ca

Random House Canada and colophon are registered trademarks.

Library and Archives Canada Cataloguing in Publication

Bates, Judy Fong, 1949–
The year of finding memory : a memoir / Judy Fong Bates.

ISBN 978-0-307-35652-9

1. Bates, Judy Fong, 1949–. 2. Bates, Judy Fong, 1949– —Family.
3. China—Biography. 4. Chinese Canadians—Biography. 5. Authors, Canadian (English)—20th century—Biography. I. Title.

Design by Terri Nimmo

Printed in the United States of America

2 4 6 8 9 7 5 3 1

for Alison and Katherine

Wheresoever you go, go with all your heart.
Confucius

I know men in exile feed on dreams of hope.
Aeschylus, from *Agamemnon*

THE MAIN CHARACTERS

FONG WAH YENT: my father and father of Hing, Shing, Jook and Doon

FONG YET LAN: my mother and mother of Ming Nee

FIRST WIFE: my father's first wife, mother of Hing, Shing, Jook and Doon

SECOND UNCLE: my father's older brother, my uncle

BIG UNCLE: my mother's oldest brother, my uncle

THOH: the Chinese title for both a sister and a daughter-in-law, the title my mother used for Big Uncle's first wife

LITTLE AUNT: my mother's younger sister, my aunt

FIRST BROTHER HING: my father's oldest son, my half-brother

SHING: my father's middle son, my half-brother

JOOK: my father's oldest daughter, my half-sister

DOON: my father's youngest son, my half-brother

MING NEE: my mother's daughter from her first marriage, my half-sister

JEN: Shing's wife, my sister-in-law

YENG: Doon's wife, my sister-in-law

KIM: Jook's oldest daughter, my niece

SU: Jook's youngest daughter, my niece

VEN: Su's husband

CHONG: Jook's youngest son, my nephew

LIANG: Jook's middle son, my nephew
LEW: First Brother Hing's son, my nephew
WEI: Lew's wife
JEEN: First Brother Hing's daughter, my niece
BING: Jeen's husband
KUNG: Little Aunt's son, my cousin
LIN: Kung's wife
MICHAEL: my husband

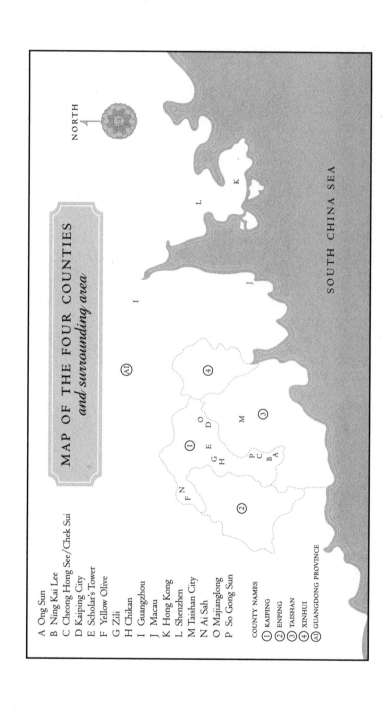

MAP OF THE FOUR COUNTIES
and surrounding area

A Ong Sun
B Ning Kai Lee
C Cheong Hong See/Chek Sui
D Kaiping City
E Scholar's Tower
F Yellow Olive
G Zili
H Chikan
I Guangzhou
J Macau
K Hong Kong
L Shenzhen
M Taishan City
N Ai Sah
O Majianglong
P So Gong Sun

COUNTY NAMES
① KAIPING
② ENPING
③ TAISHAN
④ XINHUI
Ⓐ GUANGDONG PROVINCE

NORTH

SOUTH CHINA SEA

AUTHOR'S NOTE

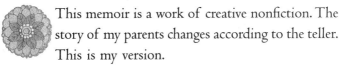 This memoir is a work of creative nonfiction. The story of my parents changes according to the teller. This is my version.

I have used the actual names of my parents and my husband. The names of many other people in this book have been changed out of respect for their privacy and, in some cases, their safety. I have also given some of the Chinese personal names new English transliterations, which I hope are closer to the Four Counties dialect.

My family is from Kaiping County, one of the counties in the region known as Sze Yup, the Four Counties (Kaiping, Taishan, Xinhui and Enping) in Guangdong Province, southern China. Many of the Chinese who immigrated to North America in the first six decades or so of the twentieth century were from this region. My family speaks Sze Yup, or Taishanese, the Four Counties dialect that is still widely spoken in the region.

Parts of this book take place in pre-Communist China.

When referring to places in China during those times, I have used the spellings that were in usage then. However, when writing about current times, I have used the Pinyin, the official system used in China for writing Chinese in the Roman alphabet.

PROLOGUE

Not long after my father hanged himself in the summer of 1972, I found a small cardboard box tucked far beneath his bed. My mother and I were clearing out his bedroom, and all that remained was this one piece of furniture. The walls needed a coat of paint, and I could see silhouettes left from pictures of family weddings and my university graduation. I knelt on the bare, wooden-planked floor and reached under with a broom handle, pulling the box toward me. I wiped away a layer of dust, and as I lifted the lid, a stagnant smell of old ink and stale papers, of things sealed off for a long time from anything living, wafted up and caught in the back of my throat.

Piled inside were several old documents, along with letters from China, written on aerograms and onion skin paper, folded and stored in airmail envelopes. I took out one of the letters and opened it, felt the thin, translucent paper between my fingers and stared at those columns of beautiful Chinese characters penned in black ink, a script that I was unable to read. What was in those letters? I wanted to know. I suddenly felt angry. In the months after my father's death, it seemed that whatever equanimity I was able to achieve could shatter in an instant. Without warning I would be seething with rage, then overcome with grief. But why was I angry again? with myself, for never learning how to read and write Chinese? for having parents so unlike me and so difficult to understand? at my father and what he had done to himself, what he had done to us?

I took a deep breath and lifted more letters out of the box. Underneath, I found my father's blue, cloth-bound Chinese passport. I found his 1949 immunization certificates for smallpox and cholera and the stub of his airline ticket from the China National Aviation Corporation—departing Hong Kong on August 22, 1949, for Gam Sun, the Gold Mountain, a place to which he had thought he would never have to return. Toward the bottom of the box, on top of some Kuomintang government bonds, was his Canadian citizenship certificate, dated July 25, 1950. On the back it stated that Fong Wah Yent was fifty-seven years old, a laundryman, five feet two inches in height, eyes brown, hair black, complexion dark and colour yellow.

I loosened a faded brown envelope from the stack of now worthless bonds. I opened it and found a green certificate with the words *Dominion of Canada* arranged in an arc of emphatic black type across the top. An ornate geometric pattern formed a border around the certificate's edge. The paper felt thick and smooth. All these things declared the importance of this document. In the lower right-hand corner, I saw a photograph of a man, a small, black-and-white portrait, similar to those in passports, except this one was on a certificate dated April 7, 1914, that had cost its holder five hundred dollars. The man was young, twenty-one years old, a year younger than I was as I sat looking at his image. His hair was parted at the side and neatly combed; his cheekbones were pronounced and his ears stuck out. He wore a dark, loose-fitting Chinese jacket with a stand-up collar. He looked back at me with an expression that was impossible to read, perhaps because the task before him was so overwhelming that he was unable to communicate an emotion. The man in the photograph was my father, and the piece of paper was his head tax certificate. How did this youth become the old man my mother found hanging from a rope in the basement of their house, the man whose death had struck us like a sudden explosion of glass, hurling shards so small and fine they embedded themselves deep in our flesh, never to be removed.

I turned this document over and saw the dates of my father's entry and re-entries clearly stamped on the back. For thirty-three years while he travelled between China and Canada, his head tax certificate reminded him that he was unwanted in this country. Two deep creases showed where the certificate had been folded into thirds so it would fit inside an envelope. Other than these signs of wear, and a few tears along the edge, it was in pristine condition, considering that it had crossed the Pacific Ocean five times. But I should not have been surprised. My parents took exceptional care of their documents, not out of pride but fear—fear that if a certain paper was lost or mutilated, they would not be allowed to enter one country or depart from another, or they would be unable to sponsor the immigration of family. Their existence would be suddenly nullified. In clean, black ink at the bottom of the certificate, covering a portion of my father's chest, was the signature of the comptroller of Chinese Immigration, Malcolm M. Reid.

My father spoke to me many times about the head tax, his voice bitter. *Only the Chinese had to pay this money. No one else. Five hundred dollars to get into this country. Five hundred dollars I had to borrow.* But until I found the head tax certificate under his bed, I was not aware that it had remained in his possession. And now I was holding it in my hand, a worthless piece of paper, a priceless document, the cost of my happiness.

I took a deep breath and continued to look at the man in this picture. The paper felt heavy and my hands were trembling. A lump grew in my throat and I struggled to swallow. For as long as I had known my father, he had been an old man. But here he was, a youth, staring at me across time itself. At that moment it seemed as if we both had our lives ahead of us. If only I could find a way into the past and warn him.

PART ONE
First Journey

ONE

I would have preferred something a little more subtle, but the pink geraniums were past their prime, the leaves beginning to brown. The red ones, however, had leaves that were new and green, with clusters of buds yet to blossom. There was a limited selection of plants at the greengrocer's, and I had walked up and down in front of the racks outside the store several times. I had contemplated other flowers this year, but for as long as I could remember, whenever my family visited the graves, they took geraniums. It was hard to know whether they had been chosen because of their low price or their symbolic value or because of superstition. Like so many rituals from my childhood, the longevity of the tradition had taken on a significance of its own, and to depart from an established way of doing things might pose a risk. We had always done it this way. And nothing bad had happened. So why change? Why risk the wrath of the gods? I picked the four best plants, and my husband put them in the back of our station wagon.

Michael and I had just picked up my brother Shing from his suburban home north of Toronto for the annual visit to my parents' graves at Mount Pleasant Cemetery. On that particular day in early June of 2006, the sky was cloudless and the air in the city felt thin. I noticed that every year, no matter which day we chose for the grave ceremony, the sun shone. I no longer bothered to check the weather forecast.

Shing is actually my half-brother, a son from my father's first marriage. He is a gentle man who possesses a quiet dignity. When he left China for Hong Kong in 1950, he was twenty years old. A year later, when he arrived in Toronto, a village uncle who owned a restaurant gave him a job as a waiter. Eventually he found a position at the post office sorting mail. He regards himself as fortunate to have a government pension that has given him and his wife a modest retirement. I have a photograph of him taken in the early fifties. Dressed in a pale summer suit, he is leaning against a shiny, black car, a beaming smile on his face. I once asked him if the car belonged to him or a friend. He laughed and said he had no idea who owned the car.

My parents' plot is marked by a pink granite headstone, with their names boldly engraved in English and Chinese. Unlike the older, established part of Mount Pleasant, where the graceful canopies of tall, elegant trees provide shade and refuge, the area where my parents are buried is like a suburb on the edge of town, with sun-baked expanses of lawn, trees and shrubs not yet mature. The graves have names like Wong, Lee, Choy, Seto and Fong.

Shing and I had filled our watering cans at the nearby tap. Michael was crouching in front of the stone, digging two holes with a trowel. As soon as he finished, he poured water into the holes and waited for it to soak in. He then removed the two geraniums from their pots and planted them. He rinsed the gravestone with the leftover water, and with a small twig he cleaned out any moss that had grown inside the engraved characters. Lastly, he pruned the conical cedar bushes on either side of the grave. Every year my husband performed this custodial role for the graves of people who weren't his parents while their children watched. Once Michael completed the tidying, my brother and I arranged the offering of oranges, dumplings and cups of tea on the grass. I had never been able to do this without thinking of it as a picnic for the dead. Shing then handed me a sheaf of spirit money, which he had purchased in Chinatown. Every colourful bill was printed with denominations in the millions and billions, money needed for bribing evil spirits in order to ensure safe passage into the afterlife. I stuffed the paper inside a large coffee tin while Shing made up three bundles of incense sticks. Michael struck a match, lit the sticks, then tossed the match into the can, igniting all those bills.

I am not a religious woman. Nevertheless, as a good Chinese daughter, I have performed these rituals every year since my father's death—but I have never left with a sense of peace, unable to escape the fact that unhappiness permeated my parents' marriage. No contented sighs over lives that had been filled with challenges but were ultimately well lived.

It was impossible not to think about their loneliness and about my father's sad end. After all these years, I still tasted a residue of shame in my mouth. As I watched Shing bow three times in front of the headstone, with the incense sticks still in his hands, I wondered if he was thinking the same thing. The memories that no one in my family dared to voice. I watched Shing as he jammed the smouldering incense into the earth next to the flowers. Was he also haunted by our father's death? Or was he thinking ahead to China, a land we had not seen for more than fifty years?

Earlier in the year, my half-sister Ming Nee, my mother's daughter from her first marriage, had proposed a family trip back to China that would include her, our brothers Shing and Doon—another son from my father's first marriage— and me. Her husband was a university professor, and through his work they had travelled frequently over the years to the Far East. She had been back to visit our family in China several times. Although Ming Nee had initiated this journey home, it turned out that she would be unable to accompany us, as our needs and her husband's schedule were incompat- ible. Nevertheless, her suggestion had planted an idea that my brothers and I could not ignore: we knew that the time had come for us to return. I wanted to be with my brothers for this homecoming, and the trip would also include Michael and Shing's wife, Jen, and Doon's wife, Yeng.

When Shing and Doon had left China, they were young men looking to the future. How vivid were those memories of growing up across the ocean? My brothers had left

14

behind in China a sister in her early twenties and an older brother in his early thirties, each married with young children. The brother was now dead and the sister was seventy-six and widowed. The last time we saw each other, I was three. It was shocking how little I knew about these half-siblings. If my sister had passed me on the street, I would not have recognized her.

Shing and Doon, though, sent money to the family in China every year. They were close in age to this sister and had grown up with her in a village I had never seen. They watched out for each other after their mother died during the Second World War and their father was stranded on the other side of the world. I knew that my role in this return journey would be peripheral. They were returning to a homeland; I would be exploring a foreign country, a place of great curiosity but no real emotional attachment. My home was here. I was a happily married woman, with a teaching career that had lasted more than twenty years and had achieved some professional success as a writer. I had raised two healthy, independent daughters, the oldest married and expecting her first child. I owned my own home. I had survived my parents' unhappy marriage and my father's tragic death. In China I would be more like my Anglo-Canadian husband—a tourist, sitting on the sidelines, watching someone else's momentous occasion.

Shing finished paying his respects and indicated to Michael and me that it was our turn to pray. I bowed three times, but I was no longer thinking about my parents. I was thinking of the deep anticipation that my brother must have felt when he first decided to make the journey to China. It was an anticipation I would never know. A twinge of envy pricked at my heart.

The food that we had set in front of the gravestone was packed away in a cooler and stored inside the station wagon, ready to take back to Shing's house. We climbed into the car and drove across the cemetery to where Second Uncle was buried. His grave is marked by a tiny, rectangular grey stone, chiselled with just his name and date of death in Chinese characters. This area has only small, flat memorial markers, and like my uncle's the inscriptions are all in Chinese. Every year we needed to wander for several minutes to find his marker because it was always overgrown with grass. But this year we found it quickly; Michael had remembered that there was a yew tree nearby, with a distinctive shape. Second Uncle had brought no children to the Gold Mountain, no son or daughter to honour his grave. Other than the fact that he was an older brother who had come to Canada with my father in the early part of the twentieth century, as a child I knew almost nothing about him, not even his name—and by the time my mother joined my father in Canada, this man had been dead for several years.

But every year Shing reminded me to buy flowers to plant for Second Uncle. I stood looking at his gravestone and thought about my parents' resting place—their upright, shining, granite headstone proudly proclaiming their status in Canada. And yet it was Second Uncle's humble marker that spoke the truth. I was only too aware of how sad and difficult my parents' lives had been in this country that remained foreign to them until they died.

꿛

On April 6, 1914, the day my father and his older brother arrived in Canada, a Vancouver newspaper, the *Daily News Advertiser*, forecast fair and warm weather. Further down the front page, the mayor of Vancouver expressed concern about the large number of Chinese who were entering the country. He emphasized the uncontrollable temper of *Orientals*, proof of their unpredictability, making them unsuitable candidates for immigration. On the same day, the *Vancouver Daily World* carried a story from a canning mill about a Chinese worker who, after being criticized by his white foreman, picked up his superior and in a fit of anger tried to throw him into a boiling cauldron. However, the Chinaman—or "Celestial" as he was called—was restrained and disaster was averted. Compared to the white Canadians, my father and the Chinese men of his generation were small. When I discovered these stories in the Vancouver newspaper archives, it was hard for me to reconcile this portrayal of a violent, impulsive Chinese man with my docile father and others like him whom I had seen over the years whenever I visited Chinatown in Toronto.

I distinctly recall from my early childhood one particular customer who came into my father's hand laundry, a giant, red-faced man who stomped through the door, stood in front of the wooden counter and banged its surface with a clenched fist until my father appeared. Waving his hand dismissively, the man leaned against the counter and boomed, "I know. No tickee, no laundree. You find, Charlie. You find." My father untied and folded back the brown paper from package after package of cleaned and pressed garments until the man recognized his clothes. He never apologized for the extra work he put my father through. And my father never protested. Instead, he nodded his head up and down, a stiff smile plastered across his face. I peeked from behind the curtain that hung over the doorway, separating the service from the washing areas. Blood rushed to my cheeks. But the next time this man came into our laundry with his sack of dirty clothes, my father wrote a name in Chinese characters on each half of the ticket before giving the man's portion to him. When the man returned for his finished laundry a few days later, again without his half of the slip, my father had to unwrap only one package. The man was speechless and managed to mutter no more than *thank you* as he left the laundry. My father later told me that he'd written the man's name on his half of the ticket.

"But he doesn't have a Chinese name," I said.

"Oh, yes, he does," said my father. "His name is Mo Noh Suk, No-Brain Uncle. I wrote it on his ticket and inside the collars of his shirts."

My father may have loathed the lowly position that he occupied in the small towns where we lived, but he never forgot it. He was meek and fearful of authority. Any anger he felt about the treatment he received from his customers and townsfolk he kept to himself. The closest he came to an act of defiance was to bestow an unflattering name in a foreign language, which he would then inscribe in black ink with a fine-nibbed pen inside their clothes. The notion that someone like my tiny father could so much as threaten, let alone attack, a *lo fon* and lift him off the ground, is so preposterous the thought of it is almost funny.

But there was, in fact, nothing funny about the way that people like my father were perceived by the *lo fons* of that time. The Chinese were considered to be undesirable, perhaps even subhuman. When I researched the records from the ship that brought my father to Vancouver, I found that passengers who were of European descent had specific destinations: cities like Calgary, Regina, Winnipeg, Toronto, Montreal; they were recognized as individuals, and as Anglican, Presbyterian, Baptist, Roman Catholic. But the Chinese passengers were a monolithic yellow horde. Every one of them was listed as a Buddhist, and regardless of where the Chinaman stepped off the train, as far as these records were concerned, he was going to Montreal, Montreal being the train's final stop.

Along with hundreds of other Chinese, my father and his older brother had travelled in steerage for three weeks across the Pacific on the *Empress of Russia*. They and their fellow countrymen were greeted by an embrace of warm, spring air and the sight of snow-capped mountains meeting the sky. But directly in front of them loomed tall white men, shouting and herding them off the ship. I can picture my father: head bent, wearing a dark, quilted jacket, gripping a bamboo suitcase in one hand, the other arm swinging, as he disembarked with all those passengers from China, huddled together, moving in a group. What did these two brothers who were going to wash clothes in the town of Timmins expect from this place that we Chinese called Gam Sun, the Gold Mountain? Surely they had heard from those who had returned to China about mistreatment at the hands of the white men. Did knowing these stories blunt the sting of the *lo fons'* disdain?

My father often talked about how hard the Canadian government made it for the Chinese to immigrate. I could tell from his tone that he resented it, but at the same time, there was a sense of resignation, as if life offered no other solution. He understood his bottom-rung position in this new world and felt powerless to do anything about it. His days had become an endless cycle of laundry: sorting, washing, ironing. If there were times he might have felt rich, they were on the return journeys to his village in China, where he would have been welcomed as a *Gam Sun huk*, a Gold Mountain guest, whose few words of English spleen, spat out in exasperation in any restaurant, would have brought the most arrogant waiter running.

It has only recently occurred to me that because my father returned to China five times, he would have seen that long stretch between Vancouver and Toronto eleven times. And yet I have no recollection of his speaking about the countryside. He never mentioned the Rockies, the Prairies or even the vastness of the land itself. I remember the first time I travelled across the country by car and my sense of awe as I discovered the immensity of this place I call home. How did the white passengers react to the group of brown-skinned men dressed in strange clothes, some of them with queues down their backs? Was there hostility, indifference or both? Did my father and his brother even look out the window of the train? Were they thinking of their homeland? Or were they already preoccupied with making themselves as unobtrusive as possible?

❧

I stood in the bright, June sunlight for a long time, contemplating Second Uncle's small, plain stone. My husband trimmed the grass around its edge and finished planting the red geraniums. Their cheerfulness felt too forced next to the dull grey marker. In the past, whenever I had visited this grave, it had been out of deference to my brother. On that particular visit, I was overcome by my own sadness. The unending loneliness of those two men's lives overwhelmed me. Michael put his arm around my shoulders.

TWO

My family made its journey from China to the Gold Mountain over a period of more than forty years. Whether my father had hoped to have his first wife and their children join him after the Great War, I do not know. The Exclusion Act of 1923 prevented him and other Chinese from sponsoring family for immigration. After the Second World War, in part because of the Chinese-Canadian contribution to the war effort, the government repealed this hateful act and allowed the Chinese to bring immediate family members across the Pacific and finally reunite.

In 1947, my father travelled back to China to marry my mother, a woman twenty years his junior, planning to spend the rest of his life in his homeland, living in comfort, surrounded by family. He was confident that the Kuomintang would prevail and continue to govern China. After the end of the war, the Communists and the Kuomintang, now no longer united against the Japanese, resumed their struggle for control of the country. But even when a Communist victory in China appeared inevitable, my father prayed for their defeat. My mother recognized the need to leave while there was still the opportunity. At her insistence, my father left China on August 22, 1949, and returned to the Gold Mountain for the last time, leaving behind his family and my mother, who was pregnant with me. Four months later, when he was fifty-seven, his last child would be born under China's new government. Ever since, my mother referred to me as a Child of the Revolution.

My father had departed with a heavy heart, realizing that a future under China's new rulers was even less predictable than one in a cold, northern land, a place where he had known only hardship and the contempt of others. Given my mother's middle-class background, her level of education and my father's status as a land owner, we would have been severely persecuted under the Communist regime. My parents would have been tortured and possibly executed, and once I was a teenager, I would have been sent out to the countryside for re-education through forced labour.

Shortly after his return to Canada my father became a Canadian citizen. He was then able to begin the arduous process of applying for permission to have eligible family members join him. According to the immigration laws of the time only spouses and single children under the age of twenty-one could be sponsored. Hing, my father's oldest son was married and in his early thirties. Jook, his daughter, was under twenty-one, but married. Because of age and marital status the government classified them both as independent and ineligible, no longer my father's responsibility. Shing, the second oldest, joined our father in 1951. My mother, Ming Nee, Doon and I fled our small market town in southern China in 1953. Between them my parents had six children. I was three years old and had no insight into the torment the adults in my family must have felt as they faced the likelihood that some of them would never see each other again. In the spring of 1955, after two years in Hong Kong, my mother and I arrived in Canada; Doon would follow a few months later. With Ming Nee's arrival in 1958, our family exodus from China ended, leaving us to live the rest of our lives on opposite sides of the world, divided by geography and politics.

For my parents, the letters that travelled back and forth across the Pacific were a lifeline connecting them to China. When they received news from home, they became excited and told me who had just married, who was ill, who had had a baby, how much everyone was suffering under the Communists. But I didn't care about the Communists. The names soon lost their faces and became meaningless sounds, forgotten the moment they were uttered. My mind was brimming with names like Helen, Susie, Jimmy, Cathy and Bobby; with stories of Cinderella, Snow White, Jack and the Beanstalk. My days were spent playing baseball, tag and hide-and-go-seek. Everything about China began to recede, cleaved from the person I was becoming.

My parents never learned to speak English. Shing and Doon both speak it poorly, and Ming Nee, who attended a few years of school in Canada, prefers to read the Chinese newspaper and to watch Chinese television, though she functions well in English. I am the only one of the family who speaks English without accent and with native-like fluency. Even though my siblings and I belong to the same family and generation, I find myself separated from them not only by our age difference, but also by education, culture, language and memory. They talk with vividness and clarity about life back in China and about our brother and sister who remained, letters linking their lives in Gam Sun to the homeland. I, however, remember almost nothing.

৵

Once my brothers and I had agreed to travel back to China together with our spouses, our next decision was the date. Spring was too wet and summer was too hot, even into the month of September. My brothers had strong memories of summers in southern China relentless with heat and oppressive humidity. So in my role as "obedient youngest sister," who negotiated with the outside world, I booked us seats on a direct flight from Toronto to Hong Kong, leaving on Friday, October 6, 2006.

The enormity of this return journey would soon have physical dimensions as well. By the time we left Toronto for China, our original party of six had expanded to include my niece Linda; my nephew Raymond; Lily, a friend of Shing's wife, Jen; Jen's aunt, Pearl; Pearl's sister, Mai; and Mai's husband, Kang—twelve people in all and more than thirty pieces of luggage, including one suitcase filled with North American ginseng and another with old clothes for our relatives back home.

Until that point, whenever I travelled abroad, I had often taken maple syrup or candy, firm in the belief that this was a natural offering from Canada. Not so, according to my sister-in-law Jen, who found my ignorance amusing. "If you're going back to China, take ginseng. That's what this country is famous for. Maybe not worth as much as the kind from Korea, but still worth a lot of money."

My mother, Fong Yet Lan, once told me her life was like a table that had been sawn in two: one half had stayed in China, the other half had been sent to Canada. I was nine, perhaps ten, when she told me this. And ever since, I have remembered the image of those two collapsed pieces of table. In my child's mind, I had imbued them with feelings; I pictured them like a Disney cartoon, both sad and comical, each failing miserably to stand upright. I yearned to bring those two stranded parts together.

In the elementary school where I attended grade five, there was a roll-down map of the world hanging over a section of the blackboard. My teacher took a pencil and made a dot near the tip of Lake Ontario that jutted out over Lake Erie. That was where we lived. Acton, Ontario, she said. But my classmates weren't paying attention; they were busy sneaking glances out the window at the falling snow. It was almost recess, and everyone was eager to put on their winter coats and boots and run outside to play. Everyone except me. While they got ready, I walked up to the map, mesmerized by this large, pink country and the tiny, black dot that represented our town. I put my finger on it, then traced up to the top of Lake Superior, across the Prairies, over the Rockies and then over the blue Pacific Ocean. I felt a knot of desperation tightening in the pit of my stomach; so much land, so much water separating our small town from the south of China, where, I had been told, it never snowed. The distance felt insurmountable. How would my mother ever bring the two halves of her table together?

We languished in Hong Kong for only two years, but in my hazy remembrance the time feels longer, another lifetime belonging to someone else. I have no memory of Doon living with us, and yet I know he did. He was in his late teens and spent his days exploring the city on his own and with other young relatives who were waiting  to emigrate. That period of my life has left me with a vague but persistent impression of that city's excitement, a memory of constantly turning my head and looking, my mother holding me by the wrist while we walked along congested sidewalks and through outdoor markets swarming with people. Often, by the end of the day, I was a sullen child.

My legs ached as I dragged my feet and followed my mother from temple to temple, walking among massive stone statues of gods, staring up at their silent faces, the air smoky and fragrant with incense, my mother making offerings, her hands clasped in prayer.

My mother clenched my hand inside hers while I struggled to keep up as we pushed our way through another noisy market until she reached a particular fortune teller. Ming Nee and I stood on either side of our mother and watched the man toss sticks into the air. He then read them after they landed on a smooth, wooden table. Once he was finished, we rushed to another clairvoyant, who released a small, white bird to choose a tiny square of folded paper with black writing on it. The writing would be interpreted by the clairvoyant, who then told my mother its meaning. I waited, holding my breath with anticipation, but hoping for what? Both times my mother handed over money, never smiling, the worry lines cutting deep furrows across her forehead. She grabbed my hand and pushed her way back through the crowds, Ming Nee following behind. Whatever it was my mother was told that day she never shared with me.

Not long after our arrival, we started to visit a family with four daughters who seemed about the same age as Ming Nee. They were from our home village and we called the mother Auntie. After my mother and I left Hong Kong, Ming Nee would live with them. She was not my father's daughter and would have to endure another three long years for our mother to attain Canadian citizenship in order to sponsor her immigration.

Then one day my mother purchased a large, hard-sided suitcase with metal clasps, and without being told, I knew that our life in Hong Kong was about to end. I watched as she filled it with dried herbal medicines; a warm, brown woollen blanket with a shiny satin binding; new clothes for me, yards of fabric; and skeins of wool. She had heard that Canada was a cold country, where the people were large, and that it would be hard for her to find clothes to fit her small frame. My mother consulted a tailor and had a navy-blue travel suit made, and she went to a beauty salon, where someone permed her hair into a nest of tight curls. All these things my mother did in preparation for our journey across the Pacific. She approached her chores methodically and without complaint. But she never smiled. On the day we left Hong Kong, she wore her new suit and a gold necklace with a heart-shaped pendant that had the word HAPPY embossed on it. I wore a gold bracelet with the letters L-U-C-K-Y linked in a chain. At the time they were only a collection of *lo fon* ABCs.

When we left for the airport in Hong Kong, my mother wept, not letting go of Ming Nee until we had to board the airplane. A tall *lo fon* stewardess ushered us into line; my mother held my hand the entire time, but her head was turned away from me. She was staring at her oldest daughter, who remained on the other side of the gate, tears streaming down her face, shoulders heaving. We stood to the side for a few moments, allowing other passengers to embark. Auntie, who had been waiting beside Ming Nee, finally led her away, and my mother and I walked through the portal. I looked up and saw my mother's face all twisted. She gripped my hand even tighter. It wasn't until I was an adult with children of my own that I began to have a real understanding of the anguish my mother must have been feeling; she was leaving behind her thirteen-year-old daughter.

My mother never touched any of the food the flight attendants brought. But for me it was an adventure, and when I first tasted tiny cubes of soft fruit floating in a small bowl of clear, sugary syrup, I thought it was delicious. There were other Chinese women on the airplane, some of whom seemed to be about my mother's age. And, like my mother, they were about to join husbands from whom they had been separated for many years. But there was one woman who I could tell was younger. Her complexion was smooth, and there was a nervousness about her. She reminded me of Ming Nee and was probably not much older. My mother said she was a mail-order bride, that she would marry her husband once she arrived. I noticed that all the women, even the mail-order bride, had their hair permed into curls, just like my mother, and that every one of them was wearing gold necklaces, bracelets and earrings.

It was night when the airplane landed in Vancouver. I remember only bright-coloured lights against a dark sky. A smiling Chinese man took a group of us on a bus, first to a hotel and then to a restaurant, where my mother ate almost nothing. The next day, we boarded another flight. This time there were fewer Chinese people on the airplane. Everybody was going to a big city, my mother told me. We were the only ones bound for a hand laundry in a small town.

The Cathay Pacific airbus was crowded with overseas Chinese. My brothers and their wives sat together in the middle aisle. The four of them had brought out their U-shaped foam supports and adjusted them around their necks in preparation for the long flight. Doon's voice kept rising with excitement, and every so often his wife, Yeng, would give him a gentle jab, telling him to lower his voice. Though it was past midnight when the airplane lifted off, the laughing and chattering did not subside for at least another hour. I was excited, but my anticipation paled next to their jubilant mood. As I sat next to my husband, I could not stop thinking about that long-ago journey in the propeller-driven plane that had taken my mother and me over the Pacific all the way from Hong Kong. I thought about the many times my father had crossed the ocean, how much my parents must have yearned for that place, both of them destined to die in a land that was never home. And for my mother, the exile was permanent, for once she left China, she never returned.

THREE

As our large group passed through Chinese immigration into Shenzhen, located on the southern border of Guangdong, my father's home province, the smooth and efficient train ride from Hong Kong became a distant memory. We found ourselves in the middle of what appeared to be a huge shopping mall, and somewhere in this massive complex, we had to find the station for the bus to Kaiping City, also in Guangdong. My sister-in-law Jen had asked a former schoolmate who now lived in Hong Kong to accompany us to Kaiping. But even Schoolmate was confused by the signs, and so were all the members of our party who could read and write Chinese. We ended up in a garage full of buses being serviced, and Shing, who is asthmatic, started to cough from the fumes.

Our party of thirteen and thirty-plus suitcases turned back and eventually went up and down one set of escalators at least three times. Simple decisions such as turning left or right became monumental and resulted in mass confusion, with some going in one direction and some going in another. Several times, we were almost run over by buses. My brothers and their wives had travelled very little since their arrival in Canada, leaving them ill equipped to negotiate new surroundings. In exasperation, Michael and I, to Jen's horror, left the group to search for the ticket booth, although neither of us knew how to speak Cantonese or read Chinese. We came back to find everyone worried that we had got lost, but all were relieved and impressed when we announced that we had found the elusive station.

The bus vibrated with loud voices, interrupted every so often by a cell phone ringing to the tune of "Happy Birthday," "Jingle Bells," "Frère Jacques" or "Für Elise." Most of the conversation was in Cantonese, but occasionally I would detect my regional dialect. And suddenly, whether I wanted to understand or not, I would know what time one voice would be arriving home, or where another knew to buy cheap underwear.

It took a long time to leave Shenzhen, a nightmare of random development, with mile after mile of shabby, concrete high rises, factories and highways. Grime coated the buildings, even the newer ones, and looking out the bus window, I saw construction sites, cranes and scaffolding everywhere. The smog blanketing the city was so thick that buildings only a short distance away soon became indistinct. Smoke from factory chimneys hung in the air, and plumes of black cloud tailed many of the vehicles on the road. There was little greenery, and the few trees we saw appeared stunted and scrawny.

I had read about China's rapid industrialization, and when I mentioned to a friend that I planned to visit my father's birth village, she had greeted my enthusiasm with cynicism. *I wouldn't expect much if I were you. That village has probably been flattened and replaced with a factory.* I had protested and said that our village was still standing; my friend shook her head, incredulous at my naïveté. But as I gazed out the window at this soul-numbing desolation, the unsettling, orange-coloured sun turning milky and incandescent behind the filthy smog, my spirits sank and I began to question if my friend had indeed been right.

But gradually we left behind the terrible urban sprawl and entered the Pearl River Delta region of Guangdong Province—an emerald landscape of low, rounded hills and wide, flat valleys covered with lush rice paddies and thick groves of sugar cane, bananas and bamboo. Bright, flowering hibiscus bushes grew along the side of the road; clumps of orange and yellow lantana and jumbled vines of blue morning glory pressed against houses. The Pearl had already fanned out into many branches, some of them wide enough for large boats to navigate. Much of the countryside had been turned into large, rectangular fish farms divided from each other by long dikes, and many of the dikes doubled as walking paths dotted with small workers' huts. Surrounding the dikes were fields full of carefully tended vegetable gardens and plantations.

But then I began to notice the apartment buildings and factories next to the fields and fish ponds. There seemed to be little concern about zoning; this was indeed a tarnished paradise. And though I couldn't imagine this place ever being anything but a source of plenty, I knew the region had suffered from both drought and floods, which throughout its history, had ruined crops and left its people starving. I pressed my forehead against the window of the bus and saw water everywhere: fish ponds, lotus ponds, streams and rivers all flowing into the mighty Pearl. Everything was fertile. Even the air seemed fecund, with its sparkling haze and humidity.

After two and a half hours on the bus, we arrived. From what I'd seen so far, Kaiping City was a scruffy industrial town, roads teeming with motor scooters, some carrying a single passenger, others an entire family, and trucks carting everything from bamboo to cages of live pigs. The curiously named Ever Joint Hotel, where we were to stay, is located on an island in the Tan Jiang River, which along with its tributaries flows through the city. The hotel is a large complex that dwarfs all the buildings in its vicinity. The moment our taxis stopped at the entrance, bell hops rushed over and opened the doors, gathered our luggage and led us through the large, glass front doors.

Inside the lobby, everyone in our group stood still. For a moment no one uttered a sound. Then there was a collective gasp. Standing in front of us and at strategic spots throughout the lobby were uniformed staff, looking ready to assist at a moment's notice. The beige marble floors and pillars dazzled our eyes, and the curved central staircase, leading to a second-floor balcony, was wide enough to fit a Cadillac. Jen had told us she'd made reservations for us at the best hotel in the area, and because of her connections via a friend of a friend, she'd been able to arrange a substantial discount. She'd assured us many times that the accommodations would be affordable. I had assumed that even though it was rated a five-star hotel, the Ever Joint would be a pale imitation of Western extravagance. I was wrong. The expressions on my brothers' faces told me that this hotel was unlike anything they had ever experienced. As we stood gawking, Jen grinned from ear to ear. I noticed a couple of *lo fon* men in suits talking to a bell hop. *Of course*, these accommodations were built for foreign business travellers and for people like us, returning to the homeland with dollars to spend.

In one corner of the lobby, a large group of Chinese sat on chairs and sofas. Some of them looked anxious, and I wondered if they were waiting for us. Our party of thirteen people was still checking in when two women approached me. One was about my age, and the other was older, with greying hair parted at the side and held in place with a bobby pin. The older one was dressed in a loose, flower-print top and pyjama-style pants. She asked, in the local Four Counties dialect spoken by my family, if I was from Canada. There was something familiar about the rhythm of her speech, an echo from my early past. I knew this strong, throaty voice. *Yes, of course.* It belonged to my sister, to Jook. "Jook Dei, Jook Dei. My older sister, Jook," I called. Without hesitation, she took me in her arms.

My sister loosened her embrace and held me at arm's length. She smiled, and the lines around her mouth and eyes deepened. I saw the years of sun and wind etched into her face. The last time I'd seen this woman, she was in her early twenties and I was a child of three. Now, more than fifty years later, I was well past middle age, with my hair turned silver, and my sister was seventy-six. This woman was once the beautiful child my father had loved and had given a poetic Chinese name meaning "Jade." My eyes grew wet with tears.

My father loved stories and language. While he worked at his hand laundry, he would compose lines of verse inside his head. He kept a book, made by sewing together cut-up sheets of brown wrapping paper, and in it he would write down his compositions, other thoughts and images that he might later use. I knew that when he bestowed this name upon my sister, he must have seen in his newborn daughter the beauty and luminescence of that precious green stone. He might not have guessed that it would be the stone's other qualities, strength and durability, that would ultimately prove more valuable. Whatever grievances we may have had about our lives in Canada paled beside the existence Jook and the rest of our family had endured under the Communist regime, most harshly during the unrest and violence of the Cultural Revolution.

My father always claimed that Jook was a great beauty and had been regarded as a prize catch, especially since he was a Gold Mountain guest, someone who could provide a good dowry. But if he had been able to predict the Communist Revolution in China, he would never have married her off. If only she had remained his responsibility. For his oldest son, Hing, it was already too late because of his age. But for his daughter . . . if only he had known. Then only one and not two of his children would have stayed in China, forever trapped by the Communists. Whenever my father told me these things, he would shake his head, his anger with life's injustices seething underneath his sigh.

Jook could not stop smiling. And the woman beside her was grinning and nodding. She seemed familiar to me, too—the way her eyes crinkled into the shape of crescent moons, the curve of her mouth when she smiled, her row of stainless-steel-capped teeth notwithstanding. "This is your niece Kim," my sister said. "You used to play together when you were children. Before you left for Hong Kong, I used to visit your mother at the family store in Cheong Hong See. You and Kim used to hold hands. I had to teach her to call you *Yee*, little aunt on mother's side." My sister explained that although I was younger, I was Kim's aunt and belonged to an earlier generation. Therefore, I had more status and the right to call her daughter by name.

I was overwhelmed by this rush of information and said, "I don't mind if Kim calls me by my name."

"No, no," said Kim, flashing her smile of silvery teeth. "I can't do that. I must respect the fact that you are of the same generation as my mother and call you by your proper title." My sister was nodding in agreement, and I saw that I would have to cast aside my Western assumptions. I was in China. Here, everyone had a place within the family and was mindful of that position.

My sister and her daughter were tall for Chinese women. They were about the same height as my brothers, and I remembered being told that my father's first wife had been tall. My sister and I smiled at each other again, neither of us believing that we were finally together. Her resemblance to our brother Doon was uncanny. But I also began to see something of our father in her. It was in the rhythm of her speech and in the way she swung one arm as she'd walked up to me. As Jook took both my hands in hers, it occurred to me that in all likelihood, no one in China knew how our father had died. No one in Canada would have written to tell them. It had remained our secret shame.

When I look at all the photos taken from that first encounter, I am reminded of the number of relatives who were at the hotel to greet us: nieces, nephews, their spouses and children. Yet I have a solid recollection only of my sister and Kim. I have no memory of my sister greeting my brothers, or of meeting Kim's husband, but the photographs show me that my memory is incomplete. I have seen pictures of all the siblings together—other photos, with various combinations of the many family members, Jook's other sons and daughter, and the adult children of First Brother Hing. And each time I come to a particular image of Jook holding Doon's hand, it catches my breath. A big sister after so many years of being apart, once more able to hold her little brother's hand in hers.

FOUR

When I returned to China, I had few facts in my possession about my Chinese history. I knew we were from Kaiping County, and I knew that Sze Yup, the Four Counties dialect I spoke with my parents, was distinct from the Cantonese that is spoken in most of the province. When my mother and I first arrived in Canada, Sze Yup was commonly spoken in Toronto's Chinatown, but as immigration patterns changed after the early 1970s, Mandarin and Cantonese began to dominate—both deemed far more urban and sophisticated. In Chinese restaurants I became reluctant to use the Sze Yup spoken in my childhood home, since I knew it would only earn me the scorn of waiters. But here in Kaiping, the dialect of my parents was everywhere, spoken by the hotel staff, the taxi drivers, the shop keepers. For the first time in my life, I felt bilingual and no longer embarrassed by my parents' language.

Beyond knowing that it was in the south of China somewhere and in Guangdong Province specifically, my understanding of Kaiping's exact location had always been fuzzy. But as soon as I unfolded a map of the Four Counties on a coffee table in the lobby of the Ever Joint Hotel, I saw how close the area was to the ocean. And that explained why this region was home to most of the Chinese who went to the Gold Mountain in the early part of the twentieth century. Just beyond the sea lay that mythical kingdom where fortunes sat waiting to be made.

I asked Kim, who was sitting beside me, to locate Ning Kai Lee, our ancestral village. She said it was too small to appear on the map. Then she picked up a pen and made a small dot south of Kaiping City. I looked for a long time at that tiny dot, the place where I was born.

❦

Over thirty people squeezed into three large vans. There was our contingent from overseas and an even larger one from China: my sister; many nieces and nephews, grown and married with children of their own; their friends; and people who happened to be going to our village and needed a ride.

On the day of our homecoming, the entire village of Ning Kai Lee was waiting for us on a paved area about the size of a tennis court. A fish pond was on one side, and the village houses were on the other. On the pavement stood wooden drying racks draped with limp, leafy green vegetables and wide, shallow baskets containing different coloured beans. The moment we arrived, one string after another of firecrackers began to explode. The villagers cheered and waved as they rushed forward and greeted my brothers and me by name. Basking in the glow of her siblings' celebrity status, Jook held my hand and announced to everyone that I was her little sister. My brothers and I had returned home from the land of milk and honey, plump with prosperity, dressed in fine clothes, sunglasses perched on our noses.

Even though it was early October, the air was hot and sticky. A constant haze seemed to magnify the sun. One of the village women stepped forward and held an open umbrella over me, concerned about the sun's rays darkening my skin. I then remembered how upset my mother became during the summer months when her complexion deepened in colour with each day of hanging laundry outside. I noticed several people staring at my Caucasian husband, who, at more than six feet, towered above everyone. Unable to contain his laughter, my brother Doon later told me that someone from the village had asked him if the *lo fon* had lost his way! It struck me that Michael was possibly the first Westerner to walk into this village, that its inhabitants had seen *lo fons* on television and in newspapers but never before in the flesh.

Many of the villagers were old, mostly women in their seventies and eighties, dressed like my sister, in variations of loose-fitting, printed cotton tops that buttoned down the front and pyjama-style pants. They were tanned and healthy, with faces and hands that revealed many years spent working in fields. All of them seemed to know the reason for our visit, and they hurried off in the same direction—toward my father's house, everyone talking at once.

A warren of tight alleyways about four or five feet wide, with an open gutter running along one side, connected the houses. The cement paths were cracked and broken along their edges. They were no longer paved with cobblestones as they were when my brothers had lived here in the thirties and forties. The older houses were made of narrow, grey bricks and fine mortar, with stone floors and clay tile roofs. Many of them were decorated with a geometric frieze of white plaster under the roof line. Although the buildings appeared weathered, it was obvious that at one time they had been beautiful in their simplicity. We walked past several vacant homes, and when I pointed them out, someone replied that all the young people had left for jobs in the city. Another voice added that it was not possible to stay and make money; it was easier to just abandon everything and go. No one wanted to live in the country when you could live in the city. Shing said that just after the war more than four hundred people lived in this village. Now there were only a hundred.

When he was a child, Doon told me, the village had no electricity. He giggled and said it wasn't like Canada. Turn on a tap and water flows. When he was a child, he went to the pond every day to fetch water, which had to be boiled before drinking. The water was unsafe, he said. You never knew what might be floating in the stream. Once, somebody had found a dead baby. I remembered how my mother would never drink water from a tap, how all her life she kept a Thermos of boiled water for drinking. Now there was a communal tap in the village, and most of the houses had at least a single light bulb attached to an electric cord dangling from the ceiling. In some homes, though, people still cooked on a hearth, using dried grass, leaves and sticks for fuel.

As I looked around, I thought about the friend who'd assumed I'd find my father's village devoured by modernization and turned into a factory or a parking lot. I smiled to myself. *Not here. Not in Ning Kai Lee.* I had wandered into a time capsule, a place largely untouched by modern life. Chickens scratched aimlessly along the paths, deserted lots had been turned into gardens and laundry hung randomly on poles between wooden supports or on string stretched between trees. The only sounds came from animals, people, the wind. After seeing the rampant industrial growth of Shenzhen, this plain village set in the midst of green, fertile fields, in spite of its poverty, felt like an Eden.

At the edge of the village, a watch tower rose above the surrounding houses. I stood back and saw that a corner of the uppermost floor had broken off. Sections of the plaster had separated from the walls, leaving bare patches of concrete. One of the villagers told me that the first floor had been removed to prevent people from climbing to the top. Of all the villages in the area, Ning Kai Lee was the poorest. Compared to the other communities, it had very few sons who'd ventured

to the Gold Mountain and thus had received very little money from abroad. Any money that had been sent from North America would have been meant for personal use—not enough to maintain a watch tower or install indoor plumbing. My father was one of the ones who went, who faithfully sent money back to the village, almost until he died.

When we reached my father's house, one of the villagers opened the two vertical halves of a weather-worn, wooden door. There were carvings of flowers across the top. Some of the panels were starting to separate, and the wooden hinges seemed loose. Everyone rushed into the first room. Against the wall was a wooden bed with a canopy and mosquito netting. Some clothes were hanging from a suspended rod, and a bicycle was parked in the corner. Someone lived here, yet no one paid any mind. I worried that we were invading this person's privacy. Then I heard someone say that a squatter lived in my father's house and that although my family still owned the house, no family member had lived there for thirty, perhaps forty, years.

The villagers funnelled through a smaller door leading deeper into the house and packed themselves into the middle room, good-naturedly pushing up against each other. All the living would have happened here, with sleeping and storage in the loft and the two small rooms on either side. The only source of light was a gap in the roof, designed to allow rain to flow into a square, recessed concrete pit in the floor and then out to the gutters in the street. But Jen noticed daylight coming through another hole in the roof, where tiles had loosened and broken away. She told my brothers and me that once we were back home, we would have to send money back for its repair. The room smelled damp, and large patches of dark mildew stained its walls. A small hearth in the corner facing us would have been used for cooking and for heat in the cooler months. In the past there would have been a table with chairs, probably in the middle of the room.

My father's house provided only shelter. There was no evidence of electricity or running water, even now. The thought of having to spend a childhood in this house made me shudder. Michael, however, was intrigued. He examined the fine mortar precisely laid between the narrow bricks and noticed how the wooden beams in the ceiling met in a perfect peak. He pointed to an old wooden washstand and remarked on its elegant proportions. And as he inspected an old ladder leaning against the wall, he said, "Look how the rungs are so perfectly fitted into the uprights." My husband asked question after question. Where did they get their fuel? Did they collect the rainwater? Where did they wash their clothes? My brothers were only too pleased to answer.

People crowded around my brothers, identifying themselves and trying to establish a past connection. Doon held a hefty roll of red yuan notes and was handing one out to each villager who came up to him. A line had actually formed, and people were waiting their turn. The room hummed with excited voices. News must have travelled that Doon Uncle was passing out money! Was it like this when my father returned each time? Was he surrounded and hailed like a homecoming hero from across the ocean?

A long sturdy beam rested on the floor next to the wall. Tightly wound twine lashed a rock securely underneath one end, and that rock sat inside a stone bowl recessed into the floor. I had never before seen anything like it. Jen must have seen the quizzical look on my face and explained that every house had such a contraption. When she was a child, she'd had to jump up and down at the opposite end of the beam from the stone, but before she was finished her explanation, Michael blurted out that it was a rice pestle. Jen didn't know those specific English words, but she smiled, delighted that this man from the West should recognize an implement that she had thought was particular to China.

On the wall above the rice pestle was something that resembled a giant fan made from a cluster of dried, broad leaves. I stood in front of it for several minutes, trying to figure out its purpose. My sister was standing behind me. "It's a cape," she said. "When we worked in the rice fields, planting and harvesting, we had to wear one just like this when it rained. Plus a wide-brimmed straw hat." Kim then lifted the cape off the wall, draped it over her back and squatted on the floor, demonstrating the motion for cutting stalks of rice, her arm moving in a fluid sweep. "We worked, just like that," my sister said, nodding and pointing at her daughter.

My brothers and my sister started to reminisce about fetching water from the stream outside the village, about gathering twigs and stalks for cooking fires, about sleeping high up in the village watch tower on hot summer nights. I listened quietly, voicing the occasional comment that would interrupt the rhythm of their shared memories. My brothers and sister never seemed to mind my little intrusions and happily answered my queries, but the moment they were finished explaining, they would carry on as if I was not there.

My father grew up with nine, or was it ten, brothers and sisters in this three-room house with two small lofts. Except for Second Uncle, who had gone with him to the Gold Mountain, I had heard very little about his other siblings. My mother had whispered something about an older sister who'd married into a nearby village and who had eventually hanged herself. Long before my father's death, she had told me in a secretive tone that his mother had also ended her life this way. She added that people in the village had said his first wife had been *ho tsu*, foul tempered, and had made his mother's life unbearable. What would I have done in such circumstances? Life in these surroundings would have been gruelling enough, never mind being bullied and hectored by a cruel daughter-in-law.

My father had been born in this village over a hundred years before. He'd lived in this house with his first wife and the children from that marriage: First Brother Hing, Shing, Jook and Doon. And almost sixty years after my father's birth, I too had been born here. The line between my current prosperity and the unrelenting poverty of my past felt tenuous and fragile. I found myself thinking about my mother coming here more than seventy years before, to teach in the local school. If it felt this isolated to me in 2006, how remote would it have felt in 1930 to a woman who had been living with her brother in the bustling city of Canton, in a mansion staffed with servants and furnished with modern comforts? My mother would have arrived in a sedan chair, carried over well-worn paths of yellow, sandy soil, not the paved, two-lane road that had brought me here. The villagers would have gathered and gawked at her, just as they had at us—an exotic creature from a distant star. But she was a young woman with a past, and perhaps this tiny, secluded community provided her with the perfect place to hide.

Partway up the largest wall of the main room in my father's house, an intricately carved wooden shrine sat on a long, wooden shelf. I looked closely and saw faint traces of gold leaf. Even a family as needy as my father's invested whatever little wealth it had into appeasing the gods. In this unadorned home, the shrine looked out of place. The remaining space on the shelf was meant for pictures of parents and grand-parents. But there were no pictures, and other than the shrine, the shelf was empty.

In anticipation of our arrival, my sister had asked one of the villagers to set up a low table underneath the shrine. My niece Kim laid out an offering for the ancestors: a cooked chicken, a piece of roast pork, some oranges and several cups of tea, a few candles and sticks of incense in a vase. A villager led Shing by the arm toward the offerings and gave him several incense sticks. After lighting them, Shing stepped before the shrine and bowed three times.

As I stood waiting for my turn, a woman tapped me on the shoulder. She was thin and bent, with a head of thick, white hair. She seemed frail, yet her voice was loud and sharp.

"The last time you were here you were *neet ei gwoy*, teeny tiny. I remember. You came with your mother and her daughter— the one who's married to a university professor. Your mother brought you here before leaving for Hong Kong. You wouldn't remember. You were still little. But I remember you, your mother and your sister."

"Y . . . you remember my mother?" I stammered. "It was so long ago."

"Everyone in the village knows about your family. Your father was a Gold Mountain guest and he hired your mother to teach at the school. She was the best teacher this village ever had. Even though she was here for only a few years, every-one still talks about her. And your father was a special man. They were both very smart people. By the time the war was over, his first wife was dead. People were not surprised when he came back and married your mother."

I stared in disbelief at this stranger who knew these private details from my parents' life. She smiled politely. Her words were opening a door. I had a persistent memory of my mother and me being taken somewhere by bicycle when I was a child. It was one of those vignettes from the past that lives on as a free-floating fragment. In my child's mind I had understood that the journey was an important one, but I did not know why. As I listened to the old woman, the scene came into focus. It wasn't a bicycle after all. I saw myself, a young child sitting on my mother's lap, with Ming Nee beside us, inside a pedicab. We were travelling from the market town where my parents had opened a store after the war. *Yes, of course!* We were returning here, to our ancestral home in this village, to where I now stood. Once again, I could see a blur of silvery spokes inside wheels turning on the dirt road. Once more, I felt the security of my mother's arms around me, the warmth and softness of her body pressed against my back, the rush of wind against my face.

Everything now made sense. My mother would not leave China without making an offering to our ancestors. She had no grasp of what life in the New World held for her. She knew, even then, that her oldest daughter would soon be left behind, while she and I would cross the Pacific to join my father. She needed all the good fortune that fate had to offer. A blessing from the ancestors was something she could not risk ignoring. I watched Shing, then Doon, as they each finished bowing before the family shrine.

When it was my turn, I carefully lit my sticks of incense and slowly bowed three times before placing them in the vase. I watched the smoke rise. On this very spot, more than fifty years ago, my mother would have stood, filled with dread, her hands clasped in prayer, appealing for the protection of our ancestors. I thought of my own life, blessed with good fortune. How wise it had been of my mother to pay her respects to the ancestors. How lucky for me.

FIVE

Although our spacious room in the five-star Ever Joint had a floor-to-ceiling window, plush carpeting and plump, upholstered chairs, the mattress, even with its thin, quilted cover, was the hardest bed my husband had ever slept on. He had difficulty adjusting to the rigid surface, but for me it brought back early childhood memories of hot summer nights in the back room of the hand laundry, lying on a low, wooden table spread with a bamboo mat. My father would sometimes sit beside me, and I listened while he told stories, some historical, others mythological, but always transporting me to a place that was far away and shrouded in mystery.

Michael was sitting at the desk, bent over, writing furiously in his black Moleskine. He was determined to keep a written record of our journey, believing photographs to be too objective, without the nuance of words. I kept a diary as well and had just finished writing about the meeting with the old woman in my ancestral village. I hadn't thought much about what she said until I saw her words written on the page.

"That old lady, in the village, she said people weren't surprised when my father came back from Canada to marry my mother. What do you think she meant by that?" I asked Michael.

"Probably nothing," he said and put down his pen. "Why?"

"It was her tone, intimating that there was something between my parents before they were married."

"Well, maybe there was."

"You don't get it," I said. My voice started to rise. "My parents didn't like each other. They married each other for practical reasons. It was like a business transaction." I suddenly felt exasperated, the words coming out sharper than I had intended. I was being unfair, of course, expecting my husband to read my thoughts. "Never mind . . . ," I muttered in a weak attempt at an apology.

The woman's words had attached themselves to my brain, and I couldn't shake them. My parents, as far as I could see, were the most unlikely couple on the face of this earth, without so much as a hint of romance between them. But if that old woman's words were true, I would have to believe that at one time my mother and father had been attracted to each other, might even have liked each other. "Impossible," I said to myself.

I met my father for the first time on a warm day in May. He was the oldest person I had ever seen. Fong Wah Yent had a deeply wrinkled face; the skin around his neck was lined and loose; a few wispy, white hairs grew on the top of his shiny, bald head; a pair of wire-rimmed glasses perched on his nose. He was a slight man, not much taller than my mother, who was less than five feet. He wore a suit that had obviously belonged to someone larger. The sleeves had been altered to fit his arm length, but the shoulders and the body of the jacket overwhelmed him.

My mother and I had arrived in Toronto the day before. An aunt and uncle from our village met us at the airport, and we spent the night with them at their house on Gerrard Street. The next day, my father came to the city by bus to take us back with him to the small town where he operated his hand laundry.

My parents had not seen each other for more than five years, and now my mother and I were in a strange country, inside a strange house, her hand holding mine in a firm grip. When my father entered the room, she stood up from the sofa where we were sitting beside each other. My parents spoke each other's names, but they did not touch. My father turned to me and said in a quiet, gentle voice, *"A nui, a sai nui,* my daughter, my little daughter." His eyes were wet. I looked down, afraid to meet the gaze of this strange man. He reached over and rested his hand on my cheek. His calloused palm felt rough against my face.

Later that afternoon he wrestled with our massive suitcase while we followed him onto a bus that would take us to Allandale, now a part of Barrie, Ontario. I sat between the window and my mother; my father sat across the aisle from us. My mother had her arm hooked through the handle of her purse. The bus drove past cows, horses and barns, but when I pointed them out to her, she wasn't interested. Every so often I heard her sigh. When I glanced over, she was biting her lower lip and twisting a handkerchief in her lap.

My father unlocked the door to his hand laundry, which occupied the first floor of a rundown building near a set of railroad tracks. The inside was dark. He reached up and pulled a string, turning on a bare light bulb attached to the ceiling. My mother and I would live with my father less than a year in this laundry, yet in my mind's eye I see it as plainly as if I was still there.

Just inside the front door, to separate the customers from the work area, was a handmade, wooden counter with a hinged top. My father lifted it and folded it back so my mother and I could walk through. We passed shelves of neatly stacked, finished laundry wrapped in brown paper, tied with string. My mother held my hand as we followed my father and the suitcase into a long, dark, narrow work space. A row of wooden laundry tubs was mounted against one wall. Long tables with layers of cloth pulled tightly over them stood in front of the opposite wall. Off to the side a door led into the windowless bedroom that I was to share with my parents. But standing in the centre of the floor was a massive machine in the shape of a barrel, encased in galvanized steel. This vessel stood horizontally on four legs inside a large metal pan, which, I later learned, would collect the water that spewed from a hose that looked to me like a tail. At the other end of the machine's round body, instead of a head, there was a wooden frame enclosing several rows of wringers that rose toward the ceiling. That first evening in my father's laundry, the shadows fell in such a way that the machine looked like a monster from a prehistoric past. I imagined this strange, mechanical creature coming alive and swallowing me into its belly.

I leaned in even closer to my mother.

My father's routine from one week to the next never varied, and my mother fell quickly into the rhythm of his work. On Saturdays and Wednesdays, my parents each sat on a wooden stool and sorted dirty clothes according to light and dark. They turned all the socks inside out and inspected under-wear for stains.

On Mondays and Thursdays, my father started the morning by lighting the small, coal-burning furnace at the base of the boiler. Within an hour hot water flowed from the taps. On other days we heated water in a large pot on the cast-iron stove. Whatever amount we ladled out for washing our faces and for dishes had to be immediately replaced.

Wash days were especially busy, my parents hurrying from one chore to another. Sorted piles of dirty clothes sat on the floor at one end of the room. Giant wicker baskets waited for wet laundry at the other. And off in a corner, pails of starch for the collars and cuffs of well-made shirts, stood ready.

My father opened the metal and wooden doors to the barrel-shaped receptacle and stuffed it with soiled laundry.

When he turned on the electric motor, the grinding of gears and the sloshing of water were so loud it was almost impossible to speak and be heard. On these days I crouched by the edge of the metal pan and watched the water as it gushed from the tail-like hose, swirling around the drain. Then, without warning, I heard my father singing long, mournful notes from some Chinese opera, his voice rising above the dreadful cacophony. But the lyrics were in classical Chinese, unlike the language we spoke in our home. For me the words were incomprehensible.

As soon as the song was finished, the corners of his mouth turned down in grim determination. My father rushed between the machine and the wooden tubs where the soapy laundry was rinsed in one tub after another until the water was clear. Next, he fed the clothes piece by piece between the rollers of a hand-cranked mangle that squeezed out all the water. The wrung-out laundry fell from the mangle in graceful, undulating curves into a wicker basket. If the weather was fine, my father hung each wet item on lines outside. At the end of the day, there were baskets stuffed with dried shirts, sheets, towels, underwear and socks, everything stiff and smelling of the sun and fresh air.

But on rainy days, and also during the winter, my father went into a room at the back of the building and packed coal into a cast-iron furnace that stood in the corner, heating the room to more than eighty degrees. He then took the wrung-out clothes and pegged everything on clotheslines strung just below the ceiling. When it was cold outside, I used to stand in that room, dressed only in panties and an undershirt, just to savour its moisture and warmth. Even on the coldest winter day, he had to open the back door, releasing clouds of billowing steam into the frosty air outside. On those rainy summer days, however, the hot furnace only added to already high temperatures. The laundry filled with humidity, and my father, dressed in dark trousers and a flimsy white singlet, dripped with perspiration.

In the winter, except for Mondays and Thursdays, when laundry was being washed, my father put off burning coal in the cast-iron stove for as long as possible, and he bundled up with a peaked cap and a bulky, shawl-collared, woollen sweater fitted over many layers of clothing. Every Tuesday and Friday, he stood from morning until night in front of his ironing table. He ironed every single article by hand, except for bed sheets, which he later put through a press with rollers. By the time my mother and I joined him, he had bought himself an electric iron. But when he first worked in a laundry, he used heavy ones that had to be warmed on the top of a coal stove. *You have to be careful,* he often told me, *because if the metal is too hot, you will scorch the shirt.* He said the lo fons grew very angry when an item of clothing was ruined, even when he offered to reimburse them. I protested and answered that the lo fons were unfair. My father shook his head and said that these accidents no longer happened. He always remembered to test the electric iron first—on the cloth that was stretched over the padded surface of the table. And he pointed to a strip along the white sheet, where arrow-shaped burn marks overlapped one another.

On ironing days, before I started school and got to know other children in the neighbourhood, I used to play in the space under my father's ironing table and watch his trousered legs shuffle back and forth. It was a space that was mine, somewhere I could create a world of my own, my parents close yet far away. I drew on sheets of brown laundry paper, cut out shapes, listened to the hiss of steam and felt the thud-glide rhythm of my father's iron pounding the padded wooden surface above my head.

The moment we set foot inside my father's hand laundry in Allandale, my mother started to complain. What was the matter with him that he chose to do business in such a god-forsaken place? She could barely stand to touch the *lo fons'* soiled belongings, and she cringed at the sour smell that permeated every fragment of their clothing. She used to stand next to the pot of boiling handkerchiefs, and as the green snot loosened and floated to the top, she shuddered and shielded her nose and mouth with one hand while she skimmed off the slime with a metal spoon. She grumbled about the lack of heat in winter and the chilblains that afflicted her hands and feet. But my father said this was nothing. She couldn't possibly know how difficult life was during his first years in Canada—the nasty *gwei doy*, ghost boys, who waited in ambush to pelt him with stones in the summer and snowballs in the winter. If he was lucky when he ventured into the streets, he was assaulted only with hateful names. His days were long hours of relentless, monotonous work; his nights were short, spent on the hard surface of an ironing table.

My mother scoffed. She had been through *the War*. The moment my mother brought up the War, I knew the quarrelling would soon crescendo. Next to the drama of the Japanese invasion of China, even my father's endless years of grinding destitution and loneliness paled. But sometimes my father tried to mount a counterattack. He talked about how he would have considered the little bit of heat he allowed us to be luxurious, how he ate only a few fermented black beans and rice—all this to save money to send back to her, to his family. My mother looked at him in disgust and told him he knew nothing about true suffering. She was the one imprisoned in this loathsome place, her *thlem gwon*, her heart and liver, ripped to shreds, forced to leave her daughter behind in Hong Kong. If only she had known ahead of time how miserable her life in the Gold Mountain would be. My mother spat out the words *Gam Sun* as if they were poison, something she had been tricked into consuming. But now it was too late. She had already made this terrible mistake.

Once my mother started to moan about her stranded daughter, my father grew silent. He was never able to contest this predicament. Except once. They were shouting at each other through the din of the washing machine. The fact that they could barely hear each other didn't seem to matter. Their quarrelling had become a drama with predictable lines that they delivered again and again, with little variation. As my father was feeding wet clothes through the electric mangle, his fingers kept coming dangerously close to the spinning rollers, and I let out a barely audible gasp of relief whenever he pulled his hand back. My worry was needless; for my father, these tasks had become so automatic he could have performed them blindfolded. And just as well. At that moment all his energy was focused on the fight he was having with my mother; each new taunt was pushing their discord to another level. Without warning he deviated from the script. He turned off the motor, and in the sudden quiet of the room, said, "If you want to go back to Hong Kong, I'll send you back. But you go alone. My daughter stays here. I will not jeopardize her future because of your stupidity."

"My stupidity? You're the one who doesn't understand."

"I said you could go back. That's what you want."

"What kind of choice is that? I would never leave my daughter. I would throw the two of us in front of a train before I left her with you. What kind of man are you? My heart and my liver already ripped from my body." My mother paused for a moment. She was standing at the kitchen table, chopping some ginger that she would later add to a stir-fry. "If I had known what it would be like here, I would never have left Hong Kong. At least there I had both my children with me."

"Do you think I love this country? You still don't understand, do you? I'm not here for me. I suffer because of my family. OPEN YOUR EYES."

"You talk to me about suffering. *I'm* the one who knows suffering." My mother was about to launch once more into her litany of wartime hardships.

"I'm sick of the arguing, your complaining," my father shouted, interrupting her. "I'm ready to cut out my tongue if you don't stop!"

My mother now had a cleaver in her hand and was about to slice some meat. Her face hardened; she rested the blade along the edge of the cutting board and glared at him, his words looming over them. My mother's voice came out cold and flat. "Cut the dead thing out. See if I care."

The arguing stopped, my mother's words suspended in the air. They each clamped their lips in silence. My father turned the motor back on, and my mother resumed her slicing. Whenever I think back on that scene between my parents, on the coincidence of my father threatening to remove his tongue while my mother stood at a chopping board with a knife in her hand, it's hard not to smile. If only my parents had been a slight bit more happy, they might have seen the irony of the situation, and perhaps laughed. If only . . .

My mother and I were with my father in Allandale for less than a year before we had to move. The landlord told my father that he was selling the building, and the new owner wanted us to leave and the machinery gone. It must have been an unsettling time for my mother. Although our home in Allandale was a grim sort of place, at least she had some contact in town with Chinese people. There was a Chinese restaurant down the street, where Doon had started working when he'd arrived a few months after my mother and me. The owner of a Chinese restaurant in Barrie visited us regularly with his wife, and they took me for drives in their large car. Once we went to a zoo, where I saw a peacock and clapped my hands with excitement when the bird fanned out its brilliant tail feathers.

My father searched in the Chinese newspaper from Toronto and found a Chinese hand laundry, fully equipped, for sale in the small town of Acton. Years later my mother would complain to me about my father's purchase. He had never consulted her about his decision to buy it. She said that if she had been in Canada for even two years at the time, she would have protested the move to Acton. She said my father should have bought a business in Toronto, where there was a Chinese community, where I would have had Chinese friends and could have gone to Chinese school. But she knew nothing about Canada. Here in this wretched country, she had become as capable as a lump of rice. Nothing at all like what she'd been in China. While we lived in Allandale and even several years after moving to Acton, she hardly ever left the laundry, never went anywhere on her own. Tasks as simple as going into a grocery store felt insurmountable.

My mother was right. We should have moved to Toronto's Chinatown. But not for my sake. For hers.

On our last day in Allandale, some men arrived to dismantle and remove the machinery. They were large and burly, smelling of sweat and unwashed clothes. My father had hired them, but he seemed so small and timid; I felt afraid. Partway through the morning, in an unwise gesture of friendship, my father gave those giant men a bottle of whiskey. It proved to be a grave mistake. The boss grinned and slapped my father on the back.

By late afternoon, the workers had dismantled the washing machine and had carted away the main components, but the floor was littered with small, greasy, metal parts. All the men, except for one, climbed into the cab of the truck. The remaining one hoisted himself into the open back. As they drove away, the man in the back waved to us, his other arm wrapped around the bottle of whiskey, a lopsided grin on his face. Even as a five-year-old child, I found my father's gift distressing. Like all children, I instinctively understood my inherent state of weakness and dependency. And because of this, even though I was not able to voice it, I realized my father's act of ingratiation stemmed not from strength but from helplessness.

The sun was low in the sky, and a long shaft of sunlight streamed through the window at the front of the laundry and streaked across the planked, wooden floor. In the semi-darkness of that room, I watched my parents, backs hunched over and movements laboured, as they picked up the scattered metal pieces and put them in cardboard boxes. They would not let me help. Every so often my mother would curse under her breath, but my father stayed silent. He didn't seem angry, yet there was something about the way he stared straight ahead, focusing on nothing, that frightened me. I wanted to cry, but didn't.

༂

Acton was only forty miles from Toronto, but in 1956 it felt far away and removed. In many ways our lives changed very little from our days at Allandale. We had no car, telephone, refrigerator or bathtub. The previous owner had left behind a two-burner hot plate on which my mother cooked all our meals. On Mondays and Thursdays my father continued to pack a cast-iron boiler with coal to heat water in preparation for the laundry. The washing machine that stood in the middle room of the first floor was like the one in Allandale. A row of wooden laundry tubs lined the wall behind it. Pushed up against the opposite wall was a kitchen table, where my mother would prepare our meals. At the back of the house was a room with clotheslines strung below the ceiling for drying clothes during inclement weather. In the parlour were the ironing tables and wooden shelves that held the finished, wrapped laundry.

The only other Chinese people in Acton at that time were a father and his two grown sons, who operated the local restaurant. For the next few years, my mother would be the only Chinese woman in the town. And I would be the only Chinese child.

We had been in Acton for over a year when my mother became friends with a woman whose husband operated a Chinese laundry in a small, nearby city. Her husband owned a car, and on Sundays the couple would drive for pleasure around the local countryside, often stopping in the little towns to visit at Chinese restaurants and laundries. My mother was pleased to finally meet someone close to her own age who was not only Chinese but also spoke our dialect. The two women liked each other, and the couple started to frequent our home. Every time they came, they encouraged us to visit them.

My mother decided that she and I would call on our new friends on a Saturday when I had no school and, being a day for sorting laundry, my father would be able to manage on his own. On the chosen morning, we put on our winter coats and boots and waited outside the five-and-dime store where the Gray Coach stopped to pick up passengers.

A half-hour later, when the bus drove into the station, I looked out the window and saw the woman's husband waiting for us. The man had a round belly and a ready smile, and as soon as he saw us stepping off the bus, he rushed over, took my hand and led us to his car, where his wife was sitting in the front seat.

The couple's laundry was on a busy street corner. He held open a heavy, wooden door with a glass window, allowing us to step inside. The air was hot and damp in contrast to the cold, crisp outdoors. The work room was filled with shiny machines that clicked and clacked as they washed, dried, pressed and folded each item. *Lo fon* girls dressed in short-sleeved blouses and knee-length skirts stood in front of these machines, passing shirts from one station to the next until each one was folded into a rectangle with a smart, cardboard bow tie tucked between the tips of the collar before the whole garment was slipped inside a cellophane bag. I stood and listened to the push of buttons, the pull of presses and the hiss of steam, these staccato rhythms so different from the harsh grinding of my father's prehistoric washing machine and the thud-glide rhythm of his iron on the pressing table. These modern machines turned out clean shirts, ready to wear, at a speed that would have been impossible for my father. He ironed almost everything by hand, then folded each smooth shirt and handkerchief so carefully, so neatly, before wrapping them up in brown paper parcels.

As the proud owner of this brand-new enterprise talked about the need to modernize and to change with the times if you wanted to make money, my mother listened with a tight-lipped smile. When he finished explaining, she sighed and nodded in agreement. She said that our family would never be rich, that we only knew the old way of doing things. Later that day the man and his wife drove us home. When this smiling, well-fed Chinese man, who also spoke proper English to his customers, stepped with us inside our laundry, I took a deep breath. The air felt colder, the rooms seemed darker, the machines more worn and my father even smaller.

༄

My family's poverty aside, I liked our home in Acton. Our bedroom was no longer on the same floor as the laundry equipment. The stairs leading to the second floor opened onto a large, square room, where my mother declared Ming Nee would sleep once she arrived. Even though an ocean and a continent separated us from my mother's daughter, it was as if she already lived with us. A pot-bellied, coal-burning stove sat in the corner of the room. Further along the wall was an empty space. My mother pointed to it and said it would be a good spot for a homework table, a place for Ming Nee to keep her books and to study. Ming Nee this, Ming Nee that. It seemed all my mother ever thought about was

Ming Nee. I was too young to understand her constant worry. I didn't know that we would wait almost another three years for her daughter to arrive. These concerns my mother never shared with me.

I was in grade one when I started to help my mother prepare for her Canadian citizenship interview. *Louis St. Laurent*, I said, enunciating clearly. *Loo-ee So Lo Lo*, my mother said, trying to mimic my sounds. Again I would repeat the name, and again I would try to correct her. It was the same process for the provinces and each capital city. I lost patience trying to teach her these Canadian facts. I was sick of having to say *British Columbia* over and over. No matter how slowly I uttered each word, it was never slow enough. And I knew she would never, not even in a million years, be able to pronounce Louis St. Laurent, the prime minister's name. I found it so easy. It frustrated me that she was unable to wrap her lips around the *lo fon* syllables. It was hopeless. But my mother was desperate to become a Canadian. Only then would she be eligible to sponsor her daughter for immigration and end their painful separation.

The laundry's previous owners had left behind a single bed and a bunk bed shoved into a small room off the larger one my mother had reserved for Ming Nee. My father and I shared the bunk, with him sleeping on the bottom bed and me on the top. A wooden bureau with three rows of drawers had also been left behind. My father used one drawer for himself; my mother and I shared the rest. The room was so tiny that I had to crouch on my father's mattress to fully open any of the drawers.

I liked the fact that we now lived on the corner of a tree-lined, residential street and that we had a backyard. And because my parents were unconcerned about the condition of our grass, it often became an after-dinner gathering spot in the summer for neighbourhood children. The year we moved to Acton, our stretch of the block was home to twenty-two children between the ages of four and nine. And at age six, I was smack in the middle.

During the warm weather, when I came out after supper, I would find several children chasing each other on our sparse,

patchy lawn. I could hear the neighbours' lawn mowers in the background and smell the fresh-cut grass. Our evenings evolved into games of tag and hide-and-go-seek. For the latter we fanned out across the entire neighbour-hood, leaning against trees, sneaking inside garages, crouch-ing behind rain barrels, then making that final mad dash, screaming *home free*. I absorbed English so quickly that by the end of the first summer, I could no longer remember a time when I didn't speak this language. I became one of the gang, united by our grass-stained clothes and sweaty bodies, breathless from chasing, shouting and laughing, the world of grown-ups far away. As the evening sun dropped, one by one my friends would start to leave, their mothers hollering their names from doorsteps. I never wanted the games to end; I always wanted to play even after the crickets had started to sing, long past dusk, deep into the dark.

The greatest pleasure of those early years in Acton was the Saturday afternoon movie at the Roxy Theatre on Mill Street. I went almost every weekend and sat inside the long auditorium with its curved ceiling, waiting for the lights to go off and for the screen at the front to light up. As the air thickened with the smell of cigarette smoke and buttered popcorn, I laughed at the zany antics of The Three Stooges, did chores on the farm with Ma and Pa Kettle and rode on horses through the Wild West with the Lone Ranger and Tonto. The movies taught me that families could be happy and that it was possible for two people to find contentment together. I learned that when a boy and girl were in love, they held hands, spoke softly and kissed gently. In fact, everything I needed to know about romance and true love I discovered at the Roxy Theatre. I was determined that I would be like the girls on that big screen, that one day I too would fall in love and get married. In my life there would be no room for a matchmaker. Under no circumstances would I be like my mother, betrothed at age three and married at age sixteen. I would not sit back and let someone else determine my future for me. I would have a boyfriend, go out on dates. I would laugh with my mouth wide open.

Her father, my mother proudly declared, was a modern man. She knew of women from "old-fashioned" families, who were only a few years older than she and had had their feet bound. But *her* father didn't believe in the custom; instead, he believed in making sure she had an education. My mother told me time and again that according to her father, a full belly was not enough, that his children must be able to read and write. But in spite of his modern ways, my grandfather still felt that it was his duty as a parent to find a suitable husband for her. My grandfather was an herbalist doctor with many rich clients, and he found a match from a particularly wealthy family for his daughter. The boy had been born, according to the local fortune teller, at a time when his stars were compatible with my mother's. Not only that, he grew up to be tall, handsome and fair skinned.

The world my mother had inhabited as a child, where marriages were arranged and a bride would not meet her husband until her wedding day, felt strange and foreign, but it captivated me. I could see her on the morning of her wedding day, trying to sit still through the hair-combing ceremony and trembling when she put on her red robe, intricately embroidered with a phoenix. I pictured her being helped into the sedan chair, head bent at a slight angle, eyes cast down, chest pounding and stomach queasy. As my mother was being carried away from her childhood home, what was she thinking? Was she hoping to live happily ever after? What if her husband was cruel? Did she weep, having to leave her family? When I was younger I used to think that if I had been in that position, I would have run away. But I now understand that like my sixteen-year-old mother, I too, would have been immo-bilized with fear. My mother said to me many times, "The moment I stepped out of the wedding sedan chair and peeked through my veil of red silk threads, I felt sick with dread."

"Why?" I asked each time, even when I knew the answer.

"My husband," she replied, "he had the eyes of a snake."

Her first husband was tall, handsome—and charming. But lurking behind his ready smile was something sinister. It didn't take long for her to find out the truth about her young hus-band: that he was already in love. But not with another woman. He was in love with the white powder, with opium.

"There were some people," my mother said, "who could smoke the white powder for occasional pleasure, but that *ho-um-ho loh*, that very no-good man, he couldn't live without it. Everything I brought in my dowry he took and sold."

In fear and desperation my mother hid her wedding gown, the last thing she owned of any value, at the bottom of the rice bin, but he found even that. I imagined my mother, a slender girl-bride, sobbing and begging her husband to stop his rampaging as he pushed and shoved furniture, searching for her gown until finally he kicked over the rice bin, shiny white grains spilling out like a river. I could hear her scream-ing *NGOY GOH, NGOY GOH—That's mine!*—the moment he uncovered that swatch of bright red silk. I could see her snatch-ing her hidden garment and pressing it to her chest while her husband bent down and pried it away from her fingers.

"That's how bad he was," my mother said every time she told the story, her voice coated with disgust. "See what a very no-good person he was? What kind of a person would sell his own wife's wedding gown?" My mother always paused and looked at me for agreement but never waited long enough for an answer. "It didn't matter that I had all the right traditions. That for my hair-combing ceremony my father invited a *good woman*, someone who was prosperous and had lots of sons. It didn't matter that she recited a good-luck poem:

First brush makes your marriage strong,
Second brush makes your lives together long,
Third brush brings you wealth and many sons to carry on.

It didn't matter that my father did all those things. You see, the stars were wrong. There was nothing my father could do about it. The gods had already decided to be unkind, giving me that very no-good man."

At this point she always let loose with a rueful laugh, signalling the end of her story. Sometimes a shake of her head followed, with a few words muttered under her breath, as if there was more to tell, probably worse, which I would never hear. A part of me never liked these stories about my parents' past lives. I didn't like the fact that both of them had been married before and that I had half-siblings who were much older, some old enough to be my parents.

When I was seven, I had a friend who told me that her mother was twenty-nine. One day we were playing at the sandbox in the park, and I saw a young, slim, dark-haired woman leaning against the corner of a picnic table. She was watching us. She was dressed in a sleeveless blouse, her long, tanned legs stretching out from a pair of short shorts. I can remember my astonishment when my friend looked up from our play and ran toward this young woman, calling her *Mummy*. It felt so unfair that she should have this mother who was so young, so pretty and feminine, while my mother seemed, well, so plain and old.

I didn't want parents who washed other people's clothes. I wanted ones who were young, with bright, sparkling smiles, who lived in a house with a flower garden and a swing set, drove a car. I wanted a father who wore a suit and worked at *the office*, a mother who stayed home and baked cookies. I wanted parents who spoke English. My parents were outsiders, people without status. Although my embarrassment shamed me, I saw how hard my father and my mother worked and how little they had. I felt their helplessness in the marrow of my bones and I hated it.

For as long as I could remember, my mother had told me how much she loved me, that I was her *thlem gwon*, her heart and her liver. Yet in the same breath, she would tell me, as if my love didn't count, that the only person who had ever loved her was her *thoh*, her sister-in-law, the one married to her oldest brother, the man I called Big Uncle. My mother was only a child of six when he'd brought this woman home as his wife. By then her own mother was dead, and it was this *thoh* who raised her. In my mother's hometown of Taishan, Big Uncle was a much celebrated man. Before he was married he had been to school in Peking, where he had passed the

Imperial Examinations. For his homecoming the entire street was festooned with red and gold banners, and the air echoed with the sound of exploding firecrackers and the smell of scorched paper. Banquets were held in his honour, and baskets of delicious cakes and biscuits were given out to neighbours. Because of that single accomplishment, many doors opened for Big Uncle. He became a high-ranking official in Chiang Kai-shek's Kuomintang army and afterwards a man of exceptional wealth. According to my mother, Big Uncle was *mung kah lah*, powerful.

I listened with rapt attention to the stories about life in Canton, living in Big Uncle's five-storey mansion, surrounded by manicured gardens and a high, wrought-iron fence, its imposing entrance guarded by a gatekeeper. Big Uncle had a staff of twelve, including servants, cooks and chauffeurs. He had built a private screening room for watching movies and a rooftop garden, where he, his family and guests would spend summer evenings sitting around a marble dining table, looking up at a star-studded sky, while servants brought out one mouth-watering course after another. The aroma of the food mingled with the fragrance of flowers redolent in the moist, night air. I could see it in my mind: the women slender and fine-boned, in their fitted silk *cheongsams*, fingernails painted, hair coiled into perfect French rolls, the men elegant in their smart, Western suits, the conversation witty, the laughter silky. Just like the movies.

It's still difficult for me to fathom the extent of Big Uncle's wealth, and my mother never told me how he made his money. As a child I never asked. But when I became an adult and aware of the corruption that was so much a part of Chinese society before the war, I grew suspicious about the source of his riches. No matter how those scenes of opulence came about, they were so beyond my experience they felt like make-believe. I was growing up in a home with no luxuries and still remember the day my father bought a television. I was eleven years old and standing beside him in the local furniture store. There were sofas, armchairs, coffee tables, china cabinets, record players and TVs, all shiny and new, carefully staged inside the showroom. In this life of mine, where I fraternized with *lo fons* and spoke only English, I had become familiar with all these things. Whenever I visited a friend from school at her house, I sat on a sofa with soft cushions. When I was invited for dinner, we sometimes ate in a dining room at a polished, wooden table. I knew to keep my elbows at my sides and how to use a knife and a fork. I looked around the store at all the new furnishings and knew that they had no effect on my father. They were so far beyond his sphere of expectation, they might as well have not been there.

The store owner smiled at us, and I told him we were looking for a television, an inexpensive one. Everyone in Acton knew who we were, and they could most likely guess our financial circumstances. The proprietor immediately took us to the back of the store. In his kindness he never offered us what we could not afford. I could tell that he was embarrassed, but there was no need for him to be apologetic. It made no difference to my father that we were taken to a back corner and shown an unwanted television with wood veneer that had turned a strange colour at best resembling blond. It made no difference that there was something wrong with the picture tube. My father cared only about the low price; the fact that no one else in town wanted it suited him just fine. When I finished translating, my father carefully counted out each necessary bill, and I booked a date for delivery.

Despite our TV's imperfect condition, I was excited and I loved it. From then on I spent much of my spare time staring at movies and programs on that black-and-white set. The picture was compressed into the bottom third of the screen, with the result that outdoor scenes always had a lot of sky, people had short legs and long torsos and every close-up revealed a face with a spectacular forehead that rose high above the squashed eyes, nose and lips. At school recesses I could finally join the discussions about the latest episode of *My Three Sons* or *The Real McCoys*. On the weekends I watched Fred Astaire dance, Judy Garland sing and Tarzan leap from branch to branch in the African jungle. It used to amuse my mother to see the Tarzan movies because she had seen them before the war at Big Uncle's house. She told me about her young nephews and how they pretended to be the ape-man, calling out while swinging on imaginary vines. Although she told me this more than once, each time it surprised me. It amazed me that this short, plump woman with permed, greying curls in a hairnet, who lived upstairs from a hand laundry, once lived in a home with servants and knew about Tarzan—something out of Hollywood, so Western, so un-Chinese. When my mother spoke about her past life, she grew aloof, and the woman I knew became mysterious and unrecognizable.

Her young husband's gambling and addiction to opium consumed his life. *What else could I do but leave?* my mother said. I wanted more details. Intuition told me that she was holding back something dark and terrible. But I was always afraid to ask. Once, though, I inquired about his parents. *Why didn't they do something?* I wanted to know. She said that his parents spoiled him and that she was just a daughter-in-law. Why should they care about her? It wasn't as if she had borne him a son. She said that the only good thing about her life was her *thoh*, who loved her and took her into the home that she and Big Uncle shared. My mother was only eighteen and newly separated from her husband. In 1930 China was still a patriarchal society and almost feudal in its attitude toward women. But my mother was determined and resourceful. And unlike many women of her generation, she knew how to read and write. It has been many years since her death, yet I still grapple with the fact that this woman, who defied the strict conventions of the time, took possession of her own future and sought shelter with the one person who truly loved her, was my mother.

While she was living with her *thoh* and Big Uncle in Canton, my mother noticed in a newspaper that a village in Kaiping County was looking for a schoolteacher, someone with a high school education. My mother applied for the position, and that is how she arrived in Ning Kai Lee.

My father had returned from Canada for the fourth time. He was a well-respected Gold Mountain guest with a reputation as a man of learning. The village made him the head of the local school's hiring committee.

My mother was a well-spoken young woman from the big city, whose brother had passed the Imperial Examinations and was now a high-ranking Kuomintang official. Her father had been an herbalist doctor; she had been schooled by the missionaries. My mother told my father all these things. That he was able to hire a woman with these qualities to teach in his humble village further elevated his status. When I was a teenager, my mother confided in me that she had never even finished high school. I asked her how she got the teaching job in the village, and she replied with a gleam in her eye, giving me a rare glimpse of her former self, "I lied." What else did she lie about? Did my father and the villagers know that she had left a husband? It seems odd that they never questioned why a woman from the city with my mother's education and social standing would want to teach in such a remote place. Did it ever occur to them that she might be concealing something?

For my mother, who had been living in a modern mansion with a host of servants in the bustling city of Canton, the village of Ning Kai Lee, with its small, simple houses could have been a painful exile. Yet whenever she spoke about this period of her life, she did so with satisfaction. She worked hard in Ning Kai Lee, but her efforts were appreciated and she felt respect.

When my father and his committee hired my mother, he would have been a man of thirty-eight who was married with three children. At this point it would be easy for me to fabricate something, to imagine that in spite of their age difference, my parents recognized each other as soul mates and fell in love, only to have to wait many years before their love could be consummated. But I don't know what that old woman I met in my father's house was thinking when she said that people in the village were not surprised that my father came back to marry my mother. The sad truth of the matter was that their eventual marriage had nothing to do with love and everything to do with survival.

Michael and I had turned off the lights in our hotel room. I was exhausted from the day's excitement and should have fallen asleep quickly. Yet I lay awake for a long time. In my mind I saw my father's plain, grey-brick house, and I smelled the mould on the walls. I saw chickens pecking in the lanes and laundry hung between trees. I saw the faded shrine in my father's house and heard the old woman with the thick, white hair telling me about my mother. I thought about my parents and the incredible distance between their past lives and the life I shared with them in that lonely hand laundry in Acton.

During my childhood, I too had lived two lives: one with my parents and one outside the laundry. We arrived in Acton from Allandale late at night on the train. It was winter, and the next day, when I went outside to play, a blue-eyed boy with yellow hair stood across the road from me and threw a chunk of ice that hit me on my mouth. I was so shocked I didn't cry, even though I was bleeding. I just stared. He glared back and called me a Chink. I burst into tears. I didn't speak very much English, but I knew it was a bad word. I hated that word Chink, but whenever I was taunted again, I kept my feelings to myself. I never told my parents about these things. Through sheer force of will, I had a happy childhood. I played with my friends, I rode my bicycle, I joined Brownies, I went to Sunday school, I was teacher's pet. Once I stepped outside my father's laundry, I was on my own, for better or for worse.

SIX

Cheong Hong See is a market town surrounded by a cluster of villages, my ancestral village, Ning Kai Lee, being one of them. During one of my father's return journeys from Canada, he purchased a corner lot in the town and built a row of three stores with an apartment on the second floor. In 1947, he and my mother opened a dry goods business in the middle space and rented out the other two. While I was growing up in Acton, I pestered my mother for stories of my early childhood, and she would tell me about how I played outside under the arcade, how I pretended to set up shop and how I filled a wicker basket with make-believe cakes before calling on Sek Lam Uncle, the tenant next door. Sek Lam Uncle and his wife had no children of their own, and they doted on me. He was a tailor, and his skills were well known throughout the area. He had a withered leg, and because of that, my mother said, tailoring was a good trade for him.

In fact, my mother often talked about this small market town. I had no memory of it and could picture it only through her stories. It never sounded grand like Big Uncle's home in Canton, but when she spoke about this place, her body would soften and contentment would fill her voice. She once told me those six years in Cheong Hong See were the best in her life, the only time she was truly happy.

"But what about when you lived in the mansion with your *thoh* and Big Uncle—all those servants and cars?" I once asked her while she was rinsing rice for our dinner.

My mother shook her head and for a moment said nothing. She poured off the cloudy water, then added more from the tap. She repeated this several times, then spread her fingers flat on top of the rice. She had taught me that if the water covered the fingers but not the top of the hand, you had the right amount. She put the pot on the burner of the hot plate and said to me, "You are young; you don't understand. It wasn't my wealth. It belonged to my brother and I was at the mercy of his good will. Yes, my *thoh* loved me, but the money belonged to my brother. The store in Cheong Hong See, though, was ours. Your father helped for a few years, and after he went back to Canada, he would send money. We were very comfortable. People from nearby villages used to stop at the store to buy things: fabric, thread, paper. But sometimes just to chat. Everyone wanted my advice, brought me letters to read and asked me to write letters for them. Not like here, where I'm good for nothing, always having to ask others for help."

Three large vans pulled up in front of the Ever Joint Hotel, where we were waiting. Each vehicle was already partially filled with family members from China and with people who were coincidentally headed in the same direction and needing a lift. The previous day we had all managed to pile inside, with some of us sitting at odd angles. I glanced at our large group from Canada. Perhaps we should have arranged for another vehicle. But once the doors opened, several of my relatives hopped out, ordered everyone inside to move over and invited us to get in. No one was worried that there were more passengers than seats. Back home I would have said something; but this was China, where vans for eight routinely carried ten or eleven. The only concession my relatives made was to my tall husband, who got to sit in the front next to the driver. In regular circumstances two people would have occupied that single bucket seat. Everyone laughed when Michael Uncle buckled his seat belt. I could not help but notice that once the van was in motion, my husband's back grew rigid and his hand gripped the door handle so tightly his knuckles blanched.

Cheong Hong See was about forty minutes outside Kaiping City. After driving some distance on the same highway that had taken us to Ning Kai Lee, we turned onto a two-lane road. Our driver leaned on the horn when passing everything from the occasional bicycle to large trucks and buses. He didn't seem particularly concerned about traffic coming in the opposite direction and tailgated as a matter of habit. Fortunately, he didn't drive very fast and the road was not too heavily travelled. The day before I'd been stuck in the middle of the van, surrounded by people and distracted by their questions and comments. I had completely missed the scenery. Today I made sure I had a window seat.

For the final stretch of the journey, we drove on a secondary road lined with eucalyptus trees, hibiscus bushes and electrical transmission towers; low-voltage power lines set off in many directions. The fields along the roadside were almost all cultivated: rice, bananas, vegetables, sugar cane, trellises heavy with melons, bamboo, papayas. But the roadside was strewn with discarded plastic bags, bottles and cellophane packaging. It was disquieting to see this beautiful landscape blighted with garbage.

Once we reached Cheong Hong See, the vans parked in front of a row of stores and everyone started to get out. My niece Kim took my hand and led me in a half walk, half run. I immediately likened the town to places I had seen in Mexico and Cuba: streets lined with decaying, two-storey buildings that had been grand in a distant past. Pillars supported a section of the second floors that projected over the sidewalks to form a shady arcade for pedestrians. Storefronts had grills and doors that rolled up to the ceiling so that no real separation existed between their interiors and the streets. People milled about, sharing the road with small motorcycles and bicycles and only a very few cars. They stopped chatting as we neared and watched this large contingent of visitors bustling through their town, so many of us unmistakably from afar. We passed a couple of men working on the motor of a tractor and, across from them, a fruit vendor sitting in the shade of an awning, her colourful produce displayed before her. The scorching temperatures had not relented since our arrival in China. The sun glowed white-hot in the sky. Holding pale blue umbrellas open above them, two women chatted as they cycled past, sunlight bouncing off the spokes of spinning wheels.

Kim and I were ahead of everyone else. Suddenly, she stopped at an intersection. Jook, who was right behind us, pointed at one of the corner buildings. "That's where you were born. There, on the second floor," my sister said.

I immediately turned to face this woman whom I had met only a few days before. What did she mean I was born here? My Canadian citizenship certificate clearly stated that I'd been born in the village of Ning Kai Lee. I wanted to correct her and told her what my certificate said. That was what our father had written. My sister made a *tsk* sound with her tongue and shook her head in exasperation. "*Heeeyah!* He's wrong. And how would he know? He was in Canada. Listen. I know. I was there."

For just a fleeting second, I saw my father's expression in my sister's face. She brushed away my protest with a few waves of her hand. There was something in her impatient gesture, in the rush of her words. I could have sworn my father was speaking from the grave. I didn't say anything for what must have seemed to Jook like a conspicuously long moment. There was no point in arguing about who was right. I took a deep breath and muttered something innocuous like "Oh, really." I had thought that we, the visitors from the Gold Mountain, were the ones with secrets. I felt a hairline crack in my certainty.

"There, up there on the second floor," Jook insisted. "Through that window." I glanced at Kim, and she shrugged her shoulders. I took a step back and surveyed this rundown, two-storey structure covered in old, flaking plaster. The rest of our party had caught up, and Jook led me by the hand into the store where my parents had managed their business. I nodded at the young couple who now rented the space from my nephew Lew, the son of First Brother Hing, who had died a few years before. Numerous shelves cluttered with cardboard boxes full of nuts and bolts, nails, keys, rivets and locks crowded the interior. Nothing was new; everything was used. Along one wall was a glass counter with a wooden frame that at one time must have been a fine piece of cabinetry. It seemed incongruous in this room so full of dusty metal sundries. Could it have belonged to my parents? I looked up and saw that the ceiling had once been decorated with a relief but was now grimy and peeling. I walked between the tight aisles several more times. What was I expecting? To see a store with thoughtfully stocked shelves and cabinets filled with carefully chosen things, a store like the one I had created in my imagination from my mother's words?

I had smiled to myself when friends in Canada said that this journey to my homeland would be a revelation. I had read about people returning to the land of their ancestors and feeling an almost mystical bond. But it seemed naïve to assume that I'd have an epiphany about myself, fill a void I didn't even know existed. My father's house in Ning Kai Lee was fascinating to explore, but the conditions in that home were medieval—so removed from my modern life, it was hard to make a connection. And this dark, junk-filled shop had nothing to do with me or who I was. If anything, I felt even more like an outsider. So why did I feel this sudden shift in the ground beneath my feet?

My husband stood in the middle of the road talking to my Canadian niece and nephew, the only two people besides me who could converse with him in English. I smiled to myself, seeing how much he stood out from everyone around him. His towering height, those large limbs and broad shoulders, his pale complexion, his face with its heavy brow and prominent Caucasian nose, his deep-set blue eyes, the light brown hair. In Acton everyone in the town knew who I was— "the little Chinese girl." When I was in grade four, a Chinese family with two school-aged children moved into the town. On the daughter's first day of school, the smiling principal brought her into my classroom. I remember how strange her straight black hair, dark, narrow eyes and brown skin seemed in a class full of faces with light hair and pale skin. I felt a flush of heat in my face and I wanted to hide behind a book. But now I was looking at my *lo fon* husband in this small market town in China, surrounded by people who had faces like mine. My *lo fon* husband, who looked happy and relaxed, without so much as a hint of discomfort. And yet I knew that I did not belong in China or in Cheong Hong See, where I had apparently been born. When my father returned, he had been a Gold Mountain guest who had come home; whereas I was a guest in China and my home was the Gold Mountain.

I stepped into the street and Doon pointed to a window on the second floor, where he had once had a bedroom. I asked Jook if it was possible to visit the apartment. She hesitated for a moment, one eyebrow rising. "Why would you go there? Nothing good to look at, just old furniture and junk," she said. As it turned out no one in the family had thought we would want to see the second floor, so no one had bothered to bring the key. Besides, I was the only one making a request. It made no sense to the others that I would travel halfway around the world to look at an unoccupied apartment in a state of disrepair. We had already made an offering at the ancestral home.

Again I noticed people staring at my husband, who was taking pictures of everything in sight. He suddenly stopped and gestured to me to come and look through the telephoto lens of his camera. I held the camera to my eye and saw a plaster frieze of flowers and leaves under the roofline of my father's building, much of the relief eroded but still lovely. Doon approached us. Apart from deteriorating because of neglect, the actual building hadn't changed that much, he said. I wished I'd seen it when it was newly built. After my mother married our father, Doon and Shing had left Ning Kai Lee with them and moved into this town. My brother pointed to the buildings across the road and said that when we'd lived here, those lots had been vacant. You could see from our corner straight to the river, where he used to fish and catch frogs, which my mother would later steam over rice.

During summer evenings in Acton, my mother often used to make a late-night soup from water, rock sugar, almonds, red dates and hard-boiled eggs. The white of the eggs would soak up the flavours from the sugar and the nuts. It was my favourite snack. But according to my mother, the best late-night treat could be had only in China: fresh frog cooked on top of rice. "Once you lifted the lid of the pot and breathed in the aroma of the steam rising from the combination of frog meat, ginger and garlic, your mouth would start to water. It's too bad you've never tasted these things. There is nothing this tasty in Canada."

I went back inside the store and tried to imagine my parents running this business together. Did they sit behind that finely crafted counter? Did my mother show customers bolts of fabric or perhaps spools of thread, buttons, sheets of writing paper? Jook came and stood beside me. "Your mother was very popular in the town. The store was very busy, and people were always stopping by to talk." Her eyes darted around, and she lowered her voice: "When our parents were here, everything was very nice, not like it is now. Your mother liked to organize things just so. She was very kind to everyone. People liked her. She was a big city girl, not like the people from around here, who never went anywhere. They were sad to see her go." My sister leaned close to me. "Your mother liked my father from the very beginning, even though he was married. People say that she chased him."

I raised my hand over my mouth in shock and stared at Jook. How could she possibly know whether my mother chased *her* father? She would have been an infant when my mother taught in the village, and when my mother left in the early thirties, Jook might have been a child of two, three at most.

"People still say that," Jook said in answer to the look of skepticism on my face. I then recalled the white-haired woman back in Ning Kai Lee, telling me that she remembered my mother, a beautiful woman, the best schoolteacher the village had ever had. I politely nodded, but secretly dismissed her comment, suspecting the woman of trying to ingratiate herself to me.

Somewhere between my suspicion and my amusement, my throat itched to correct these rumours about my parents. If only these people knew what I knew. During my childhood it seemed that *doo sut* was a sickening fact of life for the Chinese community. I had clear memories of my parents whispering to each other *doo sut, doo sut.* Such and such, you know the fellow who worked in the restaurant in that small town just north of us? He took his own life, had been found dangling from the end of a rope. It was the first time I'd heard my father refer to a *gow meng*, a dog life. I didn't know then precisely what he meant, but I knew from his bitter tone that it was something worthless, not good. Years later I remembered hearing about a cook from a Chinese restaurant in one of the nearby towns leaping off the roof of his two-storey building. Just a few weeks earlier, I had been sitting next to him at a wedding banquet in Toronto.

Jook and my other relatives in China had no inkling of what life in Gold Mountain had been like for people like her father. No idea of the deprivation, the loneliness, the racism, the homesickness. The terrible price our father paid, the permanent tangle of shame, anger, guilt and grief that he left behind for those of us in Canada. Jook and the others never saw my mother at my father's funeral, so devastated and inconsolable that she could barely walk. They assumed my parents had enjoyed a life dripping with wealth because they had sent money even to people who weren't related to them.

My sister was still nodding her head, convinced that her stories about my parents were true. In the end I swallowed the growing desire to set the record straight, and I kept my mouth shut. What was the point of divulging the truth about these people they had idealized? What would be gained by disturbing happy memories?

SEVEN

O *f all his children, my father loved me the most.* A few days before, when I first heard Jen, Shing's wife, make this announcement, I was astounded. It reminded me of my mother telling me that her *thoh* loved her more than she loved her own children. I could not imagine someone from a Western culture making this statement. As parents, as teachers, we are so careful not to indicate favouritism. Nor would a son or daughter proclaim such a thing except to cause strife. But within my sister-in-law's family, this was perceived as fact and accepted by her siblings without resentment. Jen had told me several times that her father had suffered from high blood pressure. She was sure that if he had been able to immigrate to Canada earlier and had had the benefit of Western medicine, he would still be alive. When I booked our flights to China, I did not know that my sister-in-law's village was close to Ning Kai Lee and that she would take this opportunity to visit and make an offering at her father's grave. Jen's siblings in Canada had also pooled their money so that after a ceremony at their father's burial site, she would be able to hold a banquet for their entire ancestral village.

My sister-in-law is from the village of So Gong Sun, which translates, literally, into Broomstick Mountain. Because Jook and my many nieces and nephews and their families had not been invited on this excursion, the vans were less crowded. Nevertheless, there were passengers I did not recognize, who, as on most of our trips, were either distant relatives or people who just needed a ride to the next village.

After leaving the same highway that took us to Ning Kai Lee and Cheong Hong See, we travelled over an ever-narrowing concrete road that wound through cultivated fields and bamboo groves until we ended up on a rutted dirt trail, both sides so overgrown with trees that the branches met in a cathederal-like arch over the road. The path widened as we neared the village and came to a stop on a paved forecourt, much like the one in Ning Kai Lee. There was even a pond by the village entrance and, as in Ning Kai Lee, the grey brick houses were arranged in a grid with narrow paths in between. We parked underneath two stately banyan trees with massive trunks and drooping branches from which aerial roots descended, some as fine as hair. I was surprised to see an ornate watch tower, several stories tall, in this village, which seemed even more isolated than Ning Kai Lee. As I looked around, I realized that So Gong Sun was larger and likely more prosperous than my father's village. Perhaps it had benefitted from the generosity of sons who had gone to the Gold Mountain. Michael and I walked to the base of the tower and peered through the bars of a window. It had long since fallen into a state of disrepair; all its flooring and joists had been removed. The ground floor of this once-impressive building now served as a stable for water buffalo.

The graves were far from the village; yet all the inhabitants followed us, forming a long procession down the narrow footpath. Jen had hired some men to carry several stretchers, one with a whole roast pig, the others with roasted chickens and ducks and other foods that would be presented at the offering. A smiling woman approached me as we walked and said that she had gone to school with my sister. She knew my sister lived in Canada and was married to a wealthy university professor. Several times, she mentioned that she and Ming Nee had been good friends and that she visited us at the store in Cheong Hong See, that she'd sometimes purchased thread and buttons from our store and that my mother had often given her candy as a treat. She repeated over and over how everyone in the village still remembered and respected my mother. All afternoon she walked beside me and held her umbrella over my head to shield me from the sun. The woman would have been the same age as Ming Nee, but she looked so much older. Her hair was grey and her face was deeply lined. I was embarrassed by her excessive attention. Why was she being *so* nice to me? What did she want? I was perturbed but also ashamed of my suspicions.

We walked past many fields, and Michael became fascinated with the water buffalo that were wallowing in nearby mud holes. My brothers watched in amusement whenever he stopped to take pictures. We found the unmarked graves on a small rise overlooking rice fields and groves of trees in the distance. As I gazed at the countryside around me, I wondered how many generations of people had walked on that same beaten path. I was standing in the middle of a landscape that had not changed for hundreds of years.

The hired men first took the food to her father's burial plot, then a few feet behind to her grandmother's. Jen, Shing and their daughter Linda made offerings at each grave by burning incense and spirit money. Once the ceremony was complete, the roast pig, chickens and ducks were chopped into chunks, then portioned and wrapped in newspaper before being put inside red plastic bags for the villagers. A large, steamed cake was also cut into slices and added to the bags. The undisturbed green field that had greeted us upon arrival was now littered with newspaper, plastic water bottles and plastic bags. There was no thought given to tidying the trash, and the villagers were amused when my Canadian niece and nephew collected all the plastic. The newspaper was left to blow away.

Back in So Gong Sun we convened in the meeting hall, which, like the watch tower, had been built by overseas money. Caterers had already set up banquet tables for the feast. Again, people came up one after another, trying to establish kinship, this time with my sister-in-law. One woman kept returning, telling her that they had been classmates. But Jen insisted that she had no memory of her. She had already distributed a great deal of cash, and I suppose that word of free money had circulated. It seemed that every man, woman and child in the vicinity was at this eleven-course dinner. Jen and her siblings had provided magnificently: bowls of ginseng soup; plates of chicken, duck, whole fish, shrimp, pork; bottles of rice wine. The food seemed endless. People were laughing and talking. Toward the end of the meal, some men hung a string of red firecrackers from the second-floor balcony to the ground below. Within seconds the air was vibrating with deafening explosions. Once the noise ended, Michael noticed a man filling the gas tank for a generator only a foot or so away from the fireworks. Smoke was still rising from their charred paper remnants.

The energy, almost a collective euphoria, during that banquet was unlike anything I had ever witnessed. My sister-in-law, a local girl, had gone overseas and made good. The village hailed her like a conquering heroine, her beneficence overflowing. Had it been like this each time my father returned to his village?

My brothers had organized a farewell luncheon for our family from China and Canada. It was held the next day. We sat at three separate tables, each spread with steaming dishes of food. At one table, Jook sat between Shing and Doon. Although ten people were around their table, the three of them might as well have been by themselves. I was sitting at the next table and watched them from the corner of my eye. I listened as Doon regaled the other two with a childhood story. One morning he had gone to the market with our father, and while they were visiting one of the stalls, the elastic in

Father's pants broke. According to Doon, Father had to clasp the top of his pants with one hand to keep them from falling, and he made Doon walk directly in front of him all the way back to the village. Doon gesticulated wildly and demonstrated the way he was made to walk. I was impressed with my brother's memory, his ability to embellish, his gift as a storyteller. My sister couldn't stop laughing, and I noticed once again how much she and Doon resembled each other.

All the years of separation seemed to have vanished, although this sensation would be short-lived. My brothers and their families would be leaving after the luncheon to begin a tour of China that would include Beijing, Shanghai and Guilin. One picture after another was taken. My sister and brothers were no longer young, and it was unlikely that my brothers would ever travel this far again.

Michael and I had opted not to join my brothers' tour. We would stay in Kaiping for another several days and explore the area. Jook and her daughter Kim would be our guides. I was eager to spend some extended time with my sister and to get to know Kim, a woman who was my age but whose life could not have been more different from mine.

EIGHT

Because the Pearl River Delta region was prone to flooding, many of the watch towers served as lookouts, allowing villagers to watch upstream for a rise in the water or for flooding in surrounding fields. But perhaps more importantly, from the watch tower's vantage point of often fifty feet or more, the villagers could detect the approach of bandits.

The Chinese word for bandit is *tak*. It is an aggressive word, one that is spat out, making a sound like a gunshot. Until the Communist takeover at the end of 1949, banditry in China was a fact of life. When I was a child and my parents talked about their homeland, they spoke frequently about the gangs of thieves that roamed the countryside, preying upon villages. They remembered stories about the savagery and ruthlessness of these outlaws. I can still see my father sitting at the dinner table, deliberately setting down his chopsticks beside his rice bowl. This was his cue, letting me know that what he was about to say was important. "You have no idea

how dangerous it was when I was a boy in Ning Kai Lee.
Thieves would come to the village and kidnap people, cut
off a finger and send it to the family, demanding ransom.
They had no mercy. They would burn down houses, murder."
My father would then tell me how safe and blessed I was to
be in Canada. But I knew, regardless of the bandits, that if
he had had his way, the Communists would never have taken
over and we would all be living in China.

Until the middle of the twentieth century, Chinese peasants sometimes had no alternative, especially if they were
young and without family, but to join gangs of outlaws who
roamed the hills and preyed on innocent villagers. In spite
of my father's stories, I imagined romantic, delinquent lives
led by heroes who railed against social inequalities. After all
I was familiar with the characters from the *Water Margin*,
whose stories were based on the lives of a group of Robin
Hood–like bandits who traipsed about ancient rural China,
fighting against injustices imposed on helpless peasants by
the rich and the powerful.

Fortunately, my father had not been lured by life as an
outlaw, a life that would surely have led to an early death.
He would have been ill-suited to such an existence anyway.
My father was a law-abiding man, honest to a fault. In
Acton, when he found pennies in the pockets of customers'
clothing, he would write down their names and how many
cents he had found on a sheet of paper kept inside his cash
box, reminding him to return their money. My mother
found this honesty excessive, and it made her cross. "The
lo fons don't care about a few cents. Why are you wasting

your time?" she demanded as she watched him file another IOU note.

My father shook his head and shot back, "So, you think a few extra cents will make us rich?" He never listened to her, unable to live with the thought that he may have taken something that didn't belong to him.

I was always confused by my mother's irritation. Looking back I can't help but wonder if it wasn't my father's rigid attitude that got under her skin, how in spite of his poverty, he wore his honesty like a badge, unwilling to compromise when a harmless opportunity surfaced, even while she was caught in a life of toil, indigence and obscurity.

The day after my brothers' farewell luncheon, we decided to explore Zili village, home to the most famous collection of watch towers in Kaiping County. The van we travelled in felt nearly empty. Kim, Jook and I sat in a back seat actually intended for three. My sister and niece still giggled when Michael sat down in the front, next to the driver, and buckled his seatbelt.

Some of the watch towers we saw were as high as nine storeys. My sister said that at one time they had been very common throughout the Four Counties. Many had been torn down, though, to make way for redevelopment, and a few others had collapsed from neglect. I had read that Kaiping County, nonetheless, had over eighteen hundred still standing. Kim flashed a grin of silvery teeth. "Yes, Kaiping has the most," she said, then looked at Michael and added, "A lot of *lo fons* like to visit them."

The Chinese word for watch tower is *diaolou*, an intriguing word, the literal translation being "throwing tower." Once, many years ago, Kim explained, a young woman was trapped in her village watch tower by bandits who wanted to know the whereabouts of her husband and son. Fearing that she might disclose this information under torture, she threw herself from the top floor. Kim loved this story. Her voice rose and fell dramatically, and she marvelled at the depth of the woman's love for her family. I was reminded of Bess, the landlord's daughter in the poem "The Highwayman" by the English poet Alfred Noyes. The authorities had bound her to a chair with ropes and taunted her by tying down a musket so the barrel aimed at her breast. Then they left her alone to await the arrival of the Highwayman. If she dared to pull the trigger to warn her beloved of the Redcoats' presence, she would also end her own life. But pull the trigger she did. I smiled to myself at this cross-cultural preoccupation with the ultimate sacrifice made in the name of love.

The road entering Zili village passed a large duck and goose pond on one side and women in makeshift stalls, selling bowls of noodles and rice soup, on the other. When Michael showed interest in the snacks, the women beckoned us over, but Jook and Kim hurried us away. My sister wagged her finger at me and said, "Don't buy from them. People like that always charge too much. We know where to get food."

Inside the village there were government signs that read "Major National Cultural Heritage." For the first time I saw baskets for garbage and recycling. The main part of the village consisted of houses, arranged in a familiar tidy grid, with pathways in between. These houses were constructed with the same grey brick as the ones in Ning Kai Lee, but they were larger and more elaborate, with more decorative details. Unlike the broken concrete paths in Ning Kai Lee, the ones inside this village and leading to the watch towers at the edge of the compound were made of large, dark slabs of stone, most likely slate. Just the same, the village shared traits with my father's. Here too chickens roamed outside the houses. Yet the place felt different. It smelled of money.

Most of the towers, which were built at the perimeter of the village, were closed, but we found one that was open to visitors. I noticed the windows in its lower storeys were secured with iron shutters and bars, evidence of the dangerous past and the fear that must have been in the very air the tower's inhabitants breathed. But as I climbed higher, the evidence of danger fell away, and the windows became large and unobstructed, allowing for breathtaking views into the distance. When we reached the open balcony on the top floor, we could see the village's other watch towers standing against the hazy blue sky. Once again, I was struck by the presence of water all around us: in rice fields, in lotus ponds, fish ponds, canals and streams. And the lushness of the terrain was astonishing. The bamboo grew more densely, the banana fronds wider and shinier than any I had seen before. From this perspective I could see how closely the villages were situated to each other, some only a few hundred yards apart. In the distance low, rounded mountains met the horizon.

The watch towers of Kaiping were constructed as early as the sixteenth century, though most were built in the 1920s and 1930s. These newer structures served as much more than lookout stations. Using reinforced concrete coated with a veneer of plaster, overseas Chinese erected extravagant residences. As I gazed around at the towers in Zili, I could see that at one time nearly a century ago there must have been great contests between men who'd returned home, keen to spend their new fortunes.

The owners brought back architectural influences from their sojourns abroad, and by incorporating them into the towers for all to see, they boasted about their travels to exotic places. From where we stood on the balcony, Michael pointed out Corinthian columns, Romanesque arches, cupolas shaped like minarets. The result was like something lifted from a Venetian fantasy. The interiors of these buildings were spacious and luxurious in a way that would have been inconceivable to those who dwelled below in simple homes made from narrow, grey bricks. When these towers were being built, what did the villagers think of their presence in their ancient countryside? I could imagine the awe and respect on their faces and hear the strains of envy in their gossip as they watched these ostentatious displays of wealth rise from the ground. The streets in Gam Sun must truly have been paved with gold for men to return with such riches.

Time and weather have bestowed upon these towers a certain patina and faded elegance. And in spite of their apparently strange architectural mix, they now possess an eerie beauty that feels distinctively Chinese. But as I took in the sight of these towers, I realized that they must also have been embodiments of hope. I gazed at the green paradise in the distance. My father did not share the success of the men who had left this display, though his dreams had been the same as theirs.

Doon, a self-made man with numerous properties in Canada and now comfortably retired, had once mused out loud about why our father persisted in the hand laundry, why he never modernized or opened a more lucrative business, such as a restaurant. Most of the Chinese were going to large centres such as Vancouver and Toronto. Before moving to Allandale, my father had operated laundries in impossibly isolated communities like Timmins, Pembroke and Trois-Rivières, places where the winters were long and hard, lumber and mining towns with sizable populations of single men who needed to have their clothes washed. A task normally relegated to women, laundry was emasculating work that ensured these men from the other side of the world faded into the social background, never threatening the status quo. With Chinese restaurants still relatively uncommon, my father was often the only Chinaman in town. When I think about his choices after he arrived in Canada, it becomes evident that getting rich was never a real possibility for him. He had no talent for making money. He only understood hard and gruelling work. Whatever "riches" he might have taken back to China were the result of savings squeezed from a life stripped to the bone. One light bulb on at a time; a steady diet of fermented black beans, pickled greens and rice; lighting the coal stove only when the temperature went below freezing; never a penny spent on personal pleasure.

As I stood on this opulent balcony above Zili village, I thought about the crumbling watch tower in Ning Kai Lee. I had walked around it several times, then stood back and taken it in. It had no ornamentation, nothing that manifested a foreign influence. That tower in my father's village was so small, so insignificant. If these watch towers in fact represented the goals of those who had travelled overseas, I couldn't help but think that the meagre tower symbolized my father's ambitions in Gam Sun. All those years depriving himself, those long, laborious hours, faithfully sending money back to China, never taking a holiday. It was as if my father was some kind of anachronism, belonging to the group of Chinese who had built the railway across Canada, not someone who had lived into the late twentieth century.

Sadness gripped my heart. Could it be that for our father, the inspiration to be bold and to dream big was never there in the first place?

In the teahouse where he had worked as a boy, my father must have overheard patrons tell enticing stories of riches waiting to be made in that land across the sea. He would also surely have heard about the destitution, the harsh climate and the callous *lo fons*. But what could be more difficult than the life he was already suffering in China? My grandfather had been a poorly paid schoolteacher and could not support his large family. The stories of want from my father's childhood became mantras in mine: his first pair of shoes at age nine, his first taste of sausage at age fourteen, always dressed in rags. The village had no running water or electricity. At age five his older sister took him into the fields to gather dried cow patties for fuel.

He started work in that teahouse when he was twelve years old. His days there were an endless round of scraping ashes from the hearth, scrubbing floors, dumping slop. A particularly vicious head cook scolded and often struck him without cause. Several times a day he walked back and forth from the well, balancing a yoke so heavy from the weight of the water buckets that blisters and weeping sores erupted on his shoulders. He felt fortunate if he managed four hours of sleep at night, before one of the cooks kicked him awake while it was still dark. If he stayed in China he would face only misery.

The Gold Mountain might at least provide him with a fighting chance for a better life.

When I was growing up, my parents frequently talked about the fact that my father had returned to China so many times. Because I heard the tale so often, it became one of those family facts that grew tedious and failed to have any real significance for me. "Your father poured a lot of money into fares going back and forth. All that money would have made him rich, even if he never made another cent over here," my mother used to remind me.

Whenever I asked my parents why he returned so many times, the answer was always the same: the most important thing in life is family, the most important thing is to *goo gah*, to protect your family. That refrain was drilled into me almost every day of my childhood. I can still hear my father's voice. *You must be frugal with yourself, so you can be generous with family and friends.*

It wasn't until I became an adult that I began to appreciate the magnitude of his actions, the fact that he chose to return so often when many of his peers remained overseas. Most of the *lo wah kew*, the old timers, made the journey home only once. They lingered a few years, got married and fathered a couple of children before taking a ship back to North America, separated from their families until the immigration laws relaxed after the war. Many of these men lived in Chinatowns in large cities. In spite of the racism around them, their community provided support and a sense of belonging. But my father didn't live in a city until he was an old man.

❧

Until their deaths my parents held fast to the virtue of self-deprivation. For a short time after we first met, Michael thought my mother owned only one handmade, green cotton dress. I corrected this impression and explained that she owned several dresses that were the same, but with one variation: short sleeves for summer and long sleeves for winter. By fitting all the pattern pieces on the same bolt of cloth several times, she would use less material and thus save money. Every new item of clothing I bought for her she put away for the elusive *good* occasion. Whenever I bought something for my father, he told me to return it to the store. The only time he wore a new suit was at Ming Nee's wedding, and it was purchased for him by his future son-in-law. I can still see him in that properly fitted dark grey suit, walking Ming Nee in her floor-length bridal gown down the church aisle.

Otherwise, my father's wardrobe consisted only of clothing that had been left unclaimed in the laundry—appropriated no sooner than five years after a parcel had been abandoned. Only then was he confident that the owner was unlikely to return. Once again, my mother found his honesty excessive, and this time I agreed. Unclaimed packages of laundry sat gathering dust on a corner shelf, and when my father opened them after his self-imposed period of grace, the shirts had often yellowed with age. Regardless, he would wash and iron them for himself. And if they were too large, he used expandable arm bands to hold up the sleeves, and he tucked shirttails that came below his thighs inside his pants.

Every so often an aerogram or a letter written on onion-skin paper arrived at the laundry from one of our relatives appealing for additional money. Below the foreign stamps was our address in awkwardly written English script, with smooth, flowing Chinese characters on the side. Since my parents continued to send money home despite my father's paltry earnings, the requests for more made him cross. "They think money grows on trees over here. That I just have to go and pick it, like some kind of fruit," I heard him say more than once. My parents talked about how the family in China never really understood the harshness of their lives in Canada. They had little sympathy toward each other, but when it came to the family back home, their feelings were united.

One afternoon while I was still in high school, I came home to my parents complaining about yet another entreaty for more money. I was sick of hearing these complaints, over and over. In my know-it-all teenage voice, I blurted out, "Money, money, money. All they ever write about is money! You haven't seen these people in years. Besides, you've given them so much. You don't owe them anything. Why bother?" My mother stopped what she was doing and glared at me, her eyes shining with anger and disbelief. "Don't ever say that," she said in a low, steady voice. "These people are family. You don't know how lucky you are. You're the one who has more. No matter how little we have here, it's more than what they have at home." My mother's words shamed me. In my foolishness I had overlooked how very real these people back in China were for them and had ignored the fact that perhaps their memories of China had more meaning than their lives here in Canada.

A few days earlier, I'd been visiting the home of a friend after school, and while we sat at her kitchen table with our Cokes and potato chips, she brought out a shoe box of old family photos: pictures of herself as a baby, of her mother and aunt when they were small children, of her grandparents and other relatives. I looked at my friend and I could see her face in the pictures of her mother as a child, in her grandmother and a great-aunt. I picked up a photograph of her mother and her siblings, children with tidy hair and dressed in smooth, white, lacy smocks, smiling sweetly in front of the camera. I held this slightly curled, black-and-white picture in my hand and wondered what it would be like to know my family's past, to recognize myself in someone who had lived long ago. My grandparents were all dead by the time I was born. It wasn't until after my father had died that it occurred to me that I didn't even know their names. I had never seen a picture of either of my parents as children. For that matter, there were no baby pictures of me or of any of my half-siblings. For me, life had started in Allandale. My relatives in China existed in a dark, meaningless past. At times it seemed as if there was a giant clothesline stretching across the Pacific, and my parents and my siblings were suspended at different points along the line. I was the only one who'd reached that distant shore, my feet firmly on the ground.

NINE

According to my mother, I used to peer out the window from the second floor of our store in Cheong Hong See and pray to Hin-ah-Gung, Old Heaven Uncle, to stop the rain. I was impatient to venture outside, to splash and wade in the puddles left behind. I have a faint memory of bending over with small, flat rectangles of wood in my hands and pushing away water that had gathered in the ruts on the road, then standing aside to watch the water rush back. In the shadow of that memory is another little girl, the two of us running through the sparkling, shallow pools and laughing. Was Kim the playmate I have so long remembered?

Once again, Jook and Kim joined Michael and me in a hired van. As we travelled along the rural roads, Michael asked about the rice fields, which appeared to be in various stages of growth. I translated for him and pointed out a particular paddy to my sister. She smiled and said, "That field is almost ready for harvest. I spent so many years farming, I can tell at a glance about a field, when it needs to be cut, whether in three months, two months or now." As I relayed these things to Michael, both women grinned, pleased that he was so interested in their experiences. "Everything you know is from books. Everything I know is from work. But some things you don't know because you lived in Canada. Now that you are here, I will teach you." My sister began with the different names for rice: *voh* while it's growing in the field; *guk*, when it's ready to be harvested; *mi* before it's cooked; and *fhun* once it's cooked. She made me teach Michael the different terms. When he repeated them, my sister and niece chuckled at his awkward pronunciations.

"In English," I explained, "there is only one word for all those things." She smiled, an expression of mild disbelief on her face, then took my hand in hers.

Because Jook and Kim had spent their lives as farmers, they had no pension from work, and the government offered no state support during old age. Nonetheless, Jook felt secure. She said confidently that her five children provided her necessities. For Kim, though, circumstances were far less kind. Her husband had been forced into early retirement and received only a small pension. Her son had managed to find work as a junior cook and contributed a portion of his salary each month. Several years before, her daughter had immigrated to Canada in an arranged marriage and now sent her family regular remittances. Without this money, Kim explained, life would have been impossible. She hoped that one day her son would be able to immigrate and that her daughter would eventually sponsor her and her husband to live with them in a suburb outside Ottawa. In spite of the economic improvements in China, North America was still the Gold Mountain. I wanted to tell my niece to think carefully about her desire to leave China. I wanted to tell her about the long, cold winters in Ottawa and the isolation she would no doubt endure, cut off from her community and people who spoke her own language. I had witnessed the full life that she was living in Kaiping and I wanted to warn her. But I had known her for less than a week. I decided to say nothing.

During her youth Kim had been persecuted by Red Guards and was sent for re-education through labour by working in rice paddies from early dawn to dusk. With a sad shrug of the shoulders, she said that by the time the Cultural Revolution was over, she was in her mid-twenties. The education system had been left in a state of disarray, and even if it hadn't been, it was too late for an ordinary person like her to return to school. I kept to myself the fact that while she was toiling in the fields in southern China, I was attending high school and then university, listening to Beatles music, wearing miniskirts, getting upset if the hairdresser had cut my bangs too short. She didn't need to hear about what for her would have been a life of privilege. When we were together, I was keenly aware that her fate could so easily have been mine. I could almost hear my parents whispering to me, their breath hot on the back of my neck, reminding me of my good fortune, of their many sacrifices, of the terrible world *oy kai*, back home, had become. Even if *oy kai* was where they longed to be.

೪ಾ

Kim felt a collection of watch towers at Majianglong village would interest Michael and me. It was much like the other villages we had encountered in that it had houses made of narrow, grey bricks, built on a grid of lanes and surrounded by tended fields and a stream flowing beside a paved fore-court outside the village. But what stood out and made it similar to Zili village was its prosperity. The homes were large and well maintained. In fact, this village was altogether well cared for apart from the angry red graffiti that had been smeared on the walls of the houses that stood on the perim-eter of the village. I was shocked at the writing, outraged that someone would actually vandalize something so beauti-ful. The slogans, Kim explained, had been painted by the Red Guards. Here it was more than forty years after the Cultural Revolution, and even though I could not read the weather-worn Chinese characters, they still pulsed with obvi-ous anger. The Revolutionary authorities would have perse-cuted the wealthy landowners who lived here, going so far as to execute many of them. It occurred to me that the poverty of my father's village may have ultimately saved it from the Red Guards' revolutionary zeal.

Michael and I decided to wander through the streets while Jook and Kim went to the far side of the village. As we were walking between the houses, a voice called out in English.

"Hello. Where you from?" We were both startled and turned toward the voice. A man in his seventies was standing outside a house, waving us toward him. He told us that he lived in Los Angeles and was visiting his family home in his ancestral village. After exchanging pleasantries, he invited us into his house. In some ways it was like my father's in Ning Kai Lee, made of the same bricks with thin lines of mortar between each course, but larger and grander, with windows and a proper second floor. This man was very proud of his house and spoke with a confident and expansive manner. There was something refined about him, and in my mind I had already pegged him as a business man, perhaps exporting goods from China to North America. So I was surprised to learn that he had worked as a cook in Los Angeles. Had my father been like this when he returned to his village? Had he been like this modern Gold Mountain guest, full of confidence and good humour?

Jook and Kim came looking for Michael and me and beckoned to us, so we said goodbye to our new friend and followed my sister and her daughter to the edge of the village. There they led us into a grove of star fruit trees—thirty, maybe forty, of them, the size of mature maples with drooping branches, covered with leaves and laden with fruit. Scattered about the forest floor were benches that the villagers had made from massive slabs of stone. I sat down on one of them and looked at the sunlight filtering through the tangle of dark branches and rich, green leaves, relishing the stillness and silence of the warm afternoon.

Kim then reached up and plucked a low-hanging star fruit. She grinned as she took a pocket knife out of her purse, cut up the fruit and offered a slice to her mother. They bit into their pieces at the same time, their faces puckering, then bursting into laughter. For these last few days I had been watching the ease that Kim and her mother had with each other. My sister was eighteen when her daughter was born. Yet they seemed more like sisters than Jook and I did, the way they walked, leaning into each other, whispering things, finishing each other's sentences, giggling like girlfriends. I smiled at their small pleasure and felt a pang of envy.

After my father died my mother lived for another twenty-eight years. For several months after her death, I kept noticing couples who appeared to be mother and daughter. I could always pick them out—as if a spotlight had shone on them. And even though I knew it was impolite, I stared. Once, while I stood waiting for a friend in the foyer of a busy lunchtime restaurant in downtown Toronto, my eyes wandered past the rushing waiters to a row of booths along the wall, where two women were sitting at a table. It was apparent from their age difference and resemblance to each other that they were mother and daughter. I could feel the pleasure they took in each other's company, the way they leaned against the table toward each other, perhaps sharing a joke. The daughter reached into her bag and gave her mother a gift, a book. The mother's face lit into a smile, and the two women rose and extended their arms. The mother gave her daughter a kiss on the cheek. I envied the relaxed intimacy between these two women, but more than anything else I envied their friendship.

All my adult life I had yearned to know my mother in that way, to be friends, to discuss the merits of a novel we had both read, a movie we had both seen, to go together to an art gallery, for a walk in the woods, to chat in a casual manner. These things my mother and I were never able to share. We were united only by the blood in our veins. She spoke only Chinese and lived in a world that was governed by superstition and fear of authority and plagued by memories of loss, betrayal and helplessness. As far as she was concerned, her life had ended the day she set foot on Canadian soil.

I was still staring at the two women in the restaurant when the mother turned, and for a moment our eyes met. My cheeks suddenly felt hot and I looked away, embarrassed that she had seen the naked longing on my face.

I once confided my regret to a childhood friend that I never knew my mother as a friend, as an equal. And in her kindness she reminded me that my mother and I possessed something special and unique, and in the way of all mothers, she probably knew me better than I knew myself. I never did find out what that "something special and unique" was, but her words comforted me. Still, the desire to know my mother more completely has never left. Our relationship was never able to mature beyond that of a needy mother and a dependent child. Even though she relied on me to take her to the doctor, to look after her banking, to fill out government forms, to do anything involving the English-speaking world, it remained important for her to instruct me, to laugh and point out to her friends that I didn't know the specific merits of various Chinese herbal tonic soups, hadn't mastered the intricacies of Chinese etiquette and had to ask for the title of a certain relative. In my mother's eyes I was a perennial little girl. Her insecurity in this so-called Gold Mountain was so profound that it seemed as if an admission of my independence might mean that she would lose her hold on me or, worse still, lose me altogether. Life had been so unkind she was unable to trust even the love of her own daughter. Throughout my adult life, my mother spoke to me in the way that a mother speaks to a six-year-old. "Phone your sister and tell her that you want to come for a visit," she once instructed me. "Don't forget to buy some oranges and to put them in a bag."

As if I would carry them loose, pressed against my body, and then hand them to Ming Nee one by one. Or worse, let them roll all over the floor. I knew I should have been a good daughter and simply agreed, but instead I shot back: "Do you think I'm an idiot? Of course, I'll put them in a bag." The moment the words left my lips, I regretted them.

A moment of silence passed between us. "You think you're so smart," she finally retorted. "Just because you have a university degree doesn't make me stupid."

I had so many conversations like that with my mother, my unwarranted rage held in check, never really escalating into an argument, never any real need for an apology, both of us backing down, a slightly sour taste left in my mouth.

Whenever I travelled to another country, my mother's parting words were never to wish me a good time but rather to warn me that she might die while I was away. "Go away and spend money on a holiday if you have to," she said. "But remember, I might not be here when you get back."

No one has ever loved me like my mother. But at times her protective wall of love grew so thick I never got to know the complex woman who lived on the other side.

I lifted my face toward the canopy of black branches and overlapping leaves that were etched against the bright blue sky above me. I was so far from home. I thought I had forgotten about that mother and daughter in the restaurant. But here they were, charging into my thoughts like uninvited guests. I smiled at Kim and Jook, their faces still puckered from the star fruit's astringency. Kim handed Michael and me a little wedge each. I took a small bite and grimaced. They burst into laughter.

TEN

Early one morning my mother laid a series of books out on a wooden table. Beside them she had set a cube of dried ink inside a small, blue china dish, wetted with a few drops of water to make a dark paste. She showed me how to grip the calligraphy brush with just four fingers, then place its tip into the watery paste, carefully wiping it along the porcelain lip, to remove any excess ink. She pointed to the one- and two-stroke characters in the book and demonstrated how to sweep the tip of the brush over the strokes. The volumes laid out on the table were beginning readers and calligraphy books my mother had bought from the travelling Chinese grocer who stopped once a week at our laundry in Acton. I had finished grade one, and with the summer holidays beginning, she wanted to teach me how to read and write Chinese. In an effort to please her, I completed a few pages, but I was an uncooperative student and my mother was not a strict taskmaster. It was warm outside, and I wanted to be with my friends, running, skipping rope, just being outdoors.

The thought of spending sunny mornings on the stuffy second floor of the laundry, practising a calligraphy that could be read only by my parents and the three men who owned the local Chinese restaurant felt pointless.

So, at the beginning of each July during my early elementary school years, I would devote only a few reluctant hours to learning written Chinese. After several successive summers, my mother gave up on me and reconciled herself to the fact that her daughter would never know how to read or write her parents' language. Instead, I would learn to embrace English, the language of the *lo fons*. I would read over and over again about Adam and Eve, Noah, Samson, Ruth and Naomi, Esther, David, Solomon, Cinderella, Snow White, Jack, Rapunzel, the Sleeping Beauty. My Chinese persisted as a language spoken by a child to her parents, a palette without nuance, restricted to primary colours, whereas, with English, I was beginning to discover endless subtleties. This language had claimed my soul. I was a willing captive.

I didn't give much thought to how my parents felt about this. What must it have been like to have a daughter whose mind was occupied by a culture that would remain to them forever alien and strange? But unbeknownst to them and to me, beneath my Western exterior I remained a dutiful Confucian daughter. Those age-old ideals had been a part of the very air in my father's laundry.

Several of my relatives had suggested visiting Kai Yuan Tower, built to commemorate scholars and specifically Confucius. Throughout my childhood my parents had emphasized the importance of learning. For her generation and class of Chinese women, my mother was considered well educated. My father had much less formal education but had nevertheless immersed himself in China's classical literature. As an indirect way of honouring my parents, I went to Kai Yuan Tower before returning home. I had grown up in a culture that ranked athletes and movie stars at the apex of the cultural pyramid. The notion that a shrine had been erected simply to honour learning had therefore tweaked my curiosity and stirred my admiration.

We went on a Sunday, a day off work for my niece Jeen and her husband, Bing; my nephew Lew and his wife, Wei. They would join us, along with Kim and Jook, on our final excursion in China. Because of the added passengers, Lew crouched between the back seat and the door of the van. Our driver took us through Kaiping City—along the riverbank road, where we saw many old, decrepit boats moored near the river's edge, some with plants growing out of their hulls. That morning, we saw our first traffic accident. A car had hit a bicycle and bent its back wheel. No one had been hurt, and the police were already redirecting cars and pedestrians. As usual, the traffic was heavy, but it flowed in a miraculously organic movement. Even with no stop signs and with traffic lights only at major intersections, the drivers seemed to intuitively understand a road language spoken with beeping horns that allowed them to drive and to overtake other vehicles and pedestrians in frighteningly close quarters.

Kai Yuan Tower was only a few kilometres outside the city. From the parking lot we had to walk up a steep hill, but no one in our party was panting for breath. Earlier, when I had commented on how fit they all seemed, they laughed and told me that they lived in apartment buildings without elevators and routinely walked up five or more flights of stairs several times a day. Once I reached the top of the hill, I could see factories, an expressway, smokestacks, communications towers, power lines, large buildings and bulldozed hillsides. The development looked recent and, like so much of the modernization in China, appeared to have happened without much planning. There was so much about this country that was beyond my ken. Little things. The hillside we had just climbed was strewn with trash, yet there were workers who were crouched over, weeding the grass, ignoring the plastic bags, straws, cellophane wrappers, wrinkled bits of paper and water bottles.

The tall, pagoda-style temple was dark and quiet inside. A giant statue of Confucius in flowing, classical robes stood in the centre of the room. In front of him a large, brass urn had been jammed with sticks of incense, some still burning. I gazed for a long time at the serene face of this man, whose influence on Chinese culture dated back more than two thousand years. When I was a child not a single day would go by without my father invoking words from this scholar. He talked about the importance of obedience and order, of knowing one's position in society and the family. As I grew older and more westernized, my connection to Confucian philosophy became tenuous. On the surface those assumptions of obedience and filial piety felt anachronistic and irrelevant to the culture I had adopted, one that promoted independence and challenged authority. My father's emphasis on modesty appeared to be at odds with Western society and the value it placed on being assertive. And in our home, given the friction between my parents, the peaceful order my fathered longed for felt like an impossible goal.

My father once said during dinner that of all the women who had married into his village, my mother came from the family with the most prestige. He then quickly added that he would never be so crass as to make that boast in public. Instead, he would assign her the position of number two. He grinned at me, then at my mother, with a twinkle in his eye and said that no one would dare claim number one. My mother smiled in silent agreement. She was in a rare happy mood. After three long years of separation, Ming Nee had finally arrived. A few days earlier, our village uncle in Toronto had taken my mother and me to the airport to meet her. The moment my mother saw her daughter, she ran toward her and burst into tears as they clasped each other in their arms. In the few years since I had last seen her in Hong Kong, Ming Nee had changed from a girl into a young woman. Her hair was no longer straight and parted at the side. It had been permed into soft curls, framing her face. She towered above our mother; she was wearing nylons and other grown-up clothes. For my mother the years of worry and longing over this daughter had ended. I too was overjoyed that she was here. I thought she would be the answer to my mother's unhappiness.

And now my mother and sister were sitting beside each other at the kitchen table in my father's laundry. It was a Sunday in the early spring and he had roasted a duck in the oven of the coal stove until the skin was crisp to perfection and the flesh inside was juicy and firm. Around the duck he had tucked slices of potatoes that would absorb the juices from the orange-peel-and-anise-flavoured marinade coating the bird. My mother had heaped Ming Nee's bowl with the best pieces of meat. My father sat at the head of the table in a home that was at peace, and we listened while he talked about Confucius.

I lifted my eyes once more and saw the wise, beatific face of the ancient philosopher. I planted several sticks of incense into the urn and lit them.

Nan Tower stands at a bend in the Tan Jiang River, the main river flowing through Kaiping City. This unadorned, fortified structure was built with gun slits on each floor. From this location, for one week in 1945, a group of Chinese patriots held off a fierce attack from Japanese soldiers who had come up the river by boat. Those who were still alive once the enemy captured the tower were taken prisoner, tortured and executed. Nan Tower is now a national memorial, with a statue of the war heroes at its entrance. Walking around the meticulously maintained grounds, I felt a sombre, almost religious tone that I had not yet experienced in China. Inside, a narrow staircase led to a lookout station from which we would be able to see up and down the river. Despite the holes from Japanese shells, which had been preserved as reminders of the courage of the defenders and the brutality of the enemy, the tower was structurally sound. My relatives hustled us up the stairs, insisting that Michael and I see everything at this historic site because they were so proud of the Chinese war effort.

Only Lew and Wei decided to accompany Michael and me to the top of the tower. They made a point of highlighting the damage inflicted by the Japanese. Although my nieces and nephews are all too young to have experienced the horrors of the invasion, they seem to have absorbed a collective historical memory of humiliation and defeat at the hands of China's ancient enemy. They spoke about the barbarity of the Japanese as if they had experienced it personally. I recognized that this anger and hurt had been passed on for several generations and I was not without sympathy, though I was personally ambivalent. My relatives' shared sense of belonging extended back many centuries, if not several millennia, whereas I belonged to a country inhabited by people who had left their homelands in order to make a new start, old grievances supposedly set aside. All the same, I sometimes longed for this kind of connection, even if it did occasionally ring untrue.

Kim and Jeen had gone ahead to order dinner at a restaurant down the road from the Nan Tower. When the rest of us arrived, we sat at a round table on the restaurant terrace, looking out over the Tian Jing River. The meal started with snail soup, a local specialty.

Lew and Bing had lit cigarettes and leaned back in their chairs, watching the smoke rise in plumes above their heads. We had finished our first course, and the other dishes would soon start to arrive. I looked at each of my relatives around the table and felt so pleased to have spent these last few days with them, so glad that we'd had them to ourselves. When we'd had to share our time with my brothers and their families, everything had felt so hectic—and except for Kim and my sister, I had never been able to keep track of who was who. But during these last several days, personalities had emerged. My nephew Lew was always smartly dressed, and Wei, his wife, was a slim, attractive woman who moved with a natural grace. My niece Jeen was always telling jokes. Bing, her husband, who was only moderately plump but still nicknamed Foo Loh, Fat Man, had a thick head of wiry hair that was much admired by my husband.

Below us the Tan Jiang ran slow and wide, the vegetation on either side green and abundant. The sun had almost met the horizon and was about to disappear behind the bushes growing in dark, knotted clumps on the far shore; the remaining daylight was gentle and golden. I watched fishermen in their wooden boats, the fluid movement of their arms as they cast their nets, a dance passed from father to son. I knew the China of my parents' generation no longer existed. But just maybe, if I maintained my vigilance, I might string together these fleeting moments and capture some essence of it.

The evening breeze from the water was cooling and the air felt soft against my skin. There was much laughter around the table. I felt as if I could spend the rest of my life in Kaiping. But tomorrow we would leave for Hong Kong.

ELEVEN

My mother had a photo of Big Uncle, taken as a young soldier in the Kuomintang army. The resemblance to my mother is remarkable—the same overbite, the same broad forehead and the same penetrating stare. My childhood memories of China have a womblike quality to them, free floating and seen through a watery lens. But not so of Big Uncle. Whenever photographs were sent to Acton of family gatherings in Hong Kong or Macau, I could always pick him out. If he had walked toward me on the street, I would have recognized him.

Just before the Communist takeover of China at the end of 1949, he managed to escape to Macau, a Portuguese protectorate, across the harbour from Hong Kong. When I lived in Hong Kong with my mother and Ming Nee, he visited us frequently, always dressed in a crisp suit and tie, a pair of round, wire-rimmed glasses perched on his nose, his silver hair oiled and combed back from his high forehead. Without being told, I knew that this man with the elegant manners and impeccable grooming was no ordinary person. Each time he visited, he brought a gift from the bakery: sweets or a cake inside a box tied with red string. My mother said that it was a terrible risk for Big Uncle to travel on the ferry from Macau to Hong Kong. The Communists were on the prowl for people who had fought against them, and if they caught Big Uncle, they would definitely take him back to Mainland China, where he would be thrown in jail, most certainly tortured and likely executed. And yet it seemed to me that Big Uncle often made that perilous journey. I was sheltered by my mother's love and too young to understand. But for her those years must have been an emotionally charged time. My mother and my uncle knew that once we left for Canada, they would never see each other again. The hurts they had nursed about each other had been put behind them.

Big Uncle was the oldest child in their family and twenty years older than my mother, the second-youngest. Her childhood playmate was her younger sister, who was very close in age. They went to school together and even attended a Sunday school, where missionaries taught them how to knit and crochet. There was another sister, referred to as the Family Beauty, but she was much older and had been married when my mother was still a child.

Beyond the fact that she had been my mother's childhood playmate, I had grown up knowing almost nothing about my mother's younger sister, Little Aunt. Before I left for China, I had learned that she'd died a year or two before my mother and that she had a son living in Macau. I had made plans to meet this cousin, if for no other reason than to honour my mother's memory. Since our arrival in China, I had become even more eager to meet this cousin. Jook's remarks about my mother "chasing" our father had been gnawing at me. I began to thirst for more information about my mother and wanted to hear whatever stories Little Aunt's son might have to share.

෴

The moment Michael and I stepped off the ferry that had taken us from Hong Kong to Macau, a middle-aged man and woman pushed through the crowds toward us. In his hand my cousin held a printout of a picture of me that I had emailed to him, a beaming smile on his face. Kung is a stocky man, a year younger than I. It felt strange to have a cousin who was my age. I'd become so accustomed to having siblings and cousins who were old enough to be my parents.

My cousin lives with his family in a spacious high-rise condominium in a residential area of Macau. And unlike the apartments in Kaiping, this building has an elevator. We walked through a large, open-air foyer to reach his door, locked behind a metal security grill. Inside, the cool, marble floors provided quick relief from the heat and humidity out-side. Amidst comfortable, Western-style furniture, a table in one corner held a number of pictures. I stepped closer, and Kung explained that these were photographs of his parents and his in-laws. There was one of a small woman who looked vaguely familiar and another, which needed no explanation, of Big Uncle as a young man in his soldier's uniform. In front of these sat a bowl of fruit and some sticks of incense. My cousin had set up a shrine for his ancestors. I felt a small pang of guilt and remembered all the stories I'd heard about the old timers in the first half of the century who had died overseas and had planned for their bones to be returned to their homeland for burial. Only then could they be worshipped as ancestors. I could not help but worry about the spirits of my parents. Were they in a state of limbo on the other side of the world, struggling to reach home?

Michael and I sat beside each other on the sofa. Lin, my cousin's wife, a plump, friendly woman, brought us oolong tea and a large plate of sliced fruit. I pointed to the picture of Big Uncle and mentioned that my mother used to have the same photograph.

My cousin smiled and said, "I owe everything to Big Uncle. If it were not for him, I would still be on the Mainland." In 1979, after the turmoil of the Cultural Revolution, China's attitude toward the outside world had relaxed somewhat and Big Uncle was able to sponsor Kung's immigration to Macau. Even though Kung was married with an infant daughter, he decided to leave on his own. When he first arrived in Macau, he worked at odd jobs day and night. Eventually, he bought a vending cart and started to sell food on the street. In less than two years, he had saved enough money to purchase a variety store with a small apartment for his family on the second floor. He then arranged for his wife and daughter to join him. He and Lin worked long hours every day of the year, and once they were old enough, his children also helped in the store. In time, Kung bought even more property, and he eventually brought his parents from the Mainland to live with his family. I was never certain how much Macau real estate my cousin owned, but through sheer industry, he was able to retire at age fifty-seven. I looked around at Kung's agreeable surroundings, pleased that he was finally able to reap the reward of all those years of hard work.

Kung left the living room for a moment and returned with several photo albums. He stacked them on the coffee table in front of me. I took the first one and opened it. To my astonishment I saw pictures of my family's life in Canada: me at age seven, nine, twelve; my father's seventieth birthday celebration; my sister's wedding; my brothers' weddings; my graduation from university; my mother's seventieth birthday.

But there was one black-and-white photograph I kept turning back to. It was a picture of me and my parents when I was about eight, taken by Shing on one of his visits to Acton. In the background was a flowering shrub and behind that, just out of view, a stone house. At the time I hadn't understood why my mother insisted we pose on a property that didn't belong to us. I felt uneasy, and I worried that the neighbour would come into her yard and confront us. She was an old lady who used a cane, and I was suddenly glad that she rarely ventured out of her house. She was a kind person and would not have objected to our being in her yard;

I just didn't want her to come across us unexpectedly. I was the only one who spoke English, and I wouldn't have known what to say. Once more, I examined the photo and saw a smiling, well-dressed family. I was beginning to see why my relatives had no real concept of my parents' hardships. My mother's careful chronicle of our lives in the West, although not an outright lie, had not been completely truthful.

These people knew so much about me, yet I had never even seen a photograph of any of them—or if I had, I had not bothered to take any interest. I opened a second album, this one had pictures of my cousin's family. I saw several groups of people I didn't recognize, but in one of them I picked out Big Uncle. Next to the other men in the photograph, he seemed to be of average size, something I had never discerned in the pictures that were sent to us in Acton. I'd always remembered my uncle as a tall man. His military bearing and quiet dignity had probably made him seem larger than he really was. In another photograph I noticed a small woman seated next to Kung, and I immediately recognized that this was the same familiar-looking woman whose photograph was on the shrine. It was Little Aunt. The resemblance to my mother was unmistakable. I looked up at my cousin and saw that his eyes had become moist, as had mine. "As long as she was able, your mother sent money to my mother," Kung said. "During the times of famine in China, had it not been for the overseas money, we would have starved. Every year my mother prayed for her older sister to return home. She had always wanted to see her sister before she died. She used to read your mother's letters over and over again. When they were children, they were very close."

My mother rarely talked about her younger sister. I was not aware that she had sent money at regular intervals and had no idea that these remittances actually allowed this woman and her family to eat and live. But then again, memory can be incomplete, and it is possible that whatever news my mother shared with me about her sister and her family never made an impression. Another side of my mother was beginning to reveal itself, one that perhaps my youthful self had chosen to ignore. Or one that she had long since put away.

"What a shame it was that the two sisters never saw each other again," my cousin said, shaking his head. "What a pity. What a pity."

From listening to Kung, it was clear that his family held my mother in awe. She was the one who had gone to that mythical land while they stayed behind, dependent on her good fortune to survive. In their eyes, she was the one who had been lucky.

Later in the afternoon, Kung's son, two daughters and infant grandson joined us. I had met the older daughter several years before, when she'd stayed in Canada with Ming Nee to study English at a local college. But when a woman who appeared to be in her sixties entered the apartment and was introduced as Kung's older sister, my cousin, I was at a loss for words. I had been told about Kung, a male cousin, living in Macau.

But a female cousin? Surely I had been told about her at some point? Or perhaps her name was so rarely mentioned that I never bothered to retain it. Sons are highly prized, even worshipped, in Chinese culture. But I was still surprised to have travelled halfway around the world to meet a male cousin, only to discover that he had a sister. As a Confucian daughter, I should not have been taken aback. But I was. I was from the West.

Kung and his wife took us all to a restaurant for dinner. Michael and I had decided ahead of time that we would pay for the meal. But the moment we entered the lobby and were led to a table already covered with linen and place settings, we both realized that my cousin had made prior reservations in our honour. We started with a whole roast suckling pig. After we ate the crackling with mini pancakes and hoisin sauce, the meat was taken away and sliced before being returned for the next course. The seafood was fresh out of the ocean: prawns, steamed fish, scallops, squid and abalone, everything firm and tender. We had broccoli with a sauce made from shredded dried scallops, tripe soup, sweet bean soup, biscuits, coconut pudding, noodles, fried rice, oranges, watermelon. My cousin had spared no expense. And he had made sure that his daughter who spoke English sat next to Michael.

All these relatives sat with me and my husband around the table. I had not known about any of them, except Kung and his daughter, of course, before this evening. I felt so happy, and yet despite the superb food, I found it hard to eat. There was a lump in my throat that would not go away. Throughout the evening, my newly discovered cousin, Lai Ming, Kung's sister, told me several times: "You remind me of my mother. You don't look like her. But there's something . . . something in your manner . . . ." I so wished I could have met Little Aunt. I found myself thinking about how my mother talked about her life being like a table cut in half. I should have helped her bring those two pieces together. The Pacific Ocean had always seemed such a huge obstacle. I should not have let her frugality or the busy-ness of my own life stand in the way.

Kung told me that he often visited his father's ancestral village in Taishan, another of the Four Counties, bordering Kaiping. He had built a house there, and the next time we visited, we could stay there with him and Lin. He would also take me to the house where our mothers had spent their childhood. I had not yet left for Canada, and already I wanted to return to China.

PART TWO
Home Again

Morning arrived with a bright blue sky, so unusual in a month that I always associated with low, grey clouds and damp, raw winds. Michael has always liked November, claiming that after being dazzled by the brilliant colours of autumn, the muted hues of brown and grey are almost a relief. Only after the leaves have fallen can you begin to appreciate the trees for their structure and the bark for its texture. It was Michael who introduced me to the diamond pattern in the bark of the ash, the flakiness of hornbeam, the craggy branches of the oak. My husband is a minimalist and to his mind there is nothing more beautiful than bare branches etched against a crystal blue sky.

Eager to walk down the hill, I grabbed a jacket and scarf before leaving the house. The grass was frozen and crunched beneath my feet. Partway down the slope that led to the woods, I stopped and looked at the fields around me. Our tenant farmer had harvested his crop of wheat, and I noticed that in our adjacent pumpkin patch, a few frost-damaged fruit were still clinging to their vines. The air felt cool and thin. I took a deep breath and gazed at the landscape around me. Everything was so dormant and desolate, so very different from the fertile countryside of Kaiping County where I had been only a few days before, where the weather was still warm, the trees laden with oranges and bananas, the fields luxuriant and green with stalks of rice swaying in the breeze.

I turned around and walked back up the hill to our vegetable garden and stood in front of our lifeless plants. They had been flattened by the frost, and Michael would spend the next few days pulling them out and preparing the beds for spring planting. A blue jay's squawk broke the silence. The air that only a moment ago had felt invigorating, suddenly took on a damp chill, and I tightened the scarf around my neck. The sky in the west was starting to cloud.

Michael comes from English and Irish stock. The men in his family are tall and fair. It would be difficult to imagine someone more physically unlike my small, dark father than my husband. And yet when I see Michael bent over and working in his garden, I think of my father. Whenever he turns the soil over with a shovel or weeds and thins his plants, his mouth is turned down at the corners, deep furrows gathered in his forehead. His facial expression, his total absorption in his rural oasis . . . I watch my husband, and I am suddenly transported to the backyard behind my father's laundry.

During our early years in Acton, milk was delivered throughout the town on a horse-drawn wagon. Whenever the horse stopped in front of our house and left a gift of *road apples*, my father would rush out with a pail and shovel, scooping up his treasure. He would then mix the manure with soil before spreading it in around his backyard crop of Chinese vegetables.

My husband and I now live a couple of hours' drive outside of Toronto in a stone house that is over 150 years old, on a hundred rolling acres with spectacular views of the countryside. It's almost a quarter of a mile from the road to our house, this long lane giving us a priceless seclusion. In the few years that we've been here, Michael has added flowers and trees to our rural retreat. The property came with a large, rectangular vegetable garden, and in the first season, he grew rows of tomatoes, potatoes, squash, eggplant, peppers, lettuce and beans. Since then, he's built new raised beds, reminiscent of the ones my father shaped, like the ones we saw in China. Every spring since we moved here three years ago, our tenant farmer has dropped off a truckload of cow manure next to Michael's gardens, and for the rest of the day, my husband can't stop grinning at his good fortune. When my father died in the summer of 1972, I had known Michael for only a short while, but I have often asked myself, if my father had lived, would these two very different men have become friends through their love of these simple pleasures.

Since Acton was one of the last towns on his route back to Chinatown in Toronto, the Chinese travelling grocer usually pulled up in front of my father's hand laundry late in the evening. In the winter he always finished his cigarette before coming inside, where he would sit for a few minutes by the coal stove and chat, sipping a cup of tea before taking our order. But during warm summer evenings, he and my parents would sit outside on our front lawn, my mother and father taking a rare break from their chores.

The back of his truck was like a storeroom on wheels, the shelves inside piled high with pungent-smelling groceries. Anticipating his arrival, my parents would make a list of all the things we would need: rice, soya sauce, herbal medicine, tofu, salted fish, Chinese sausage, pressed duck. For the first few years that we lived in Canada, until I discovered Halo shampoo, my mother used to buy an herbal mixture that she boiled in a pot of water. Once the dark brew had cooled, she poured it into a basin and used it to rinse our hair. Each week I was allowed to buy a box of my favourite preserved licorice plums, wrapped in crinkly, translucent paper.

Every year in early December, the Chinese grocer sold my father bulbs called *sui sin fah*. After my father nestled them among smooth stones inside glass bowls filled with water, my parents would wait for them to sprout slender, green stalks, and when the buds blossomed into clusters of small, white, star-shaped flowers, their sweet perfume filling the room, they would smile with pleasure. Some years later I learned that they were paper whites—narcissus—and that *sui sin fah* meant "clear water flower." I've continued this tradition in my own home. And I now find myself wondering if I do so not just because of the beauty of these delicate flowers, but also because of my memory of a rare moment of shared delight between two unhappy people.

When I look back on my childhood, those bulbs seem like such an unlikely purchase—something that could not be eaten or worn, something without any practical use. Everything in our home was utilitarian. Our first kitchen table my father made by hammering together some scraps of wood. After we had been in Acton for a few years, a family in the neighbourhood gave us their unwanted red Arborite table. When we finally got a sofa, it was from the same family, who were replacing the old battered one that had sat for many years on their veranda. I don't recall my parents spending so much as a penny on anything that might add beauty or comfort to our home. The closest thing we had to art was a Chinese movie star calendar given to us by the travelling grocer. I never gave those narcissus bulbs much thought when I was a child. But as I look back I cannot help but wonder if these dainty white flowers were purchased not just because they were a harbinger of spring, of warm days to come, but because they were a reminder of China.

My father turned over the soil in his garden every spring. In our backyard he had made a row of about a dozen small, oblong raised beds. Before planting he spent hours squatting next to the beds, making sure the sides were sloped at a particular angle. He raked the tops of those beds until the soil was broken and free of lumps, then randomly scattered seeds across the surface for vegetables grown by no one else in town.

From branches and scrap wood, he fashioned a trellis that supported his peas and tied the vines with strips of torn cloth. Every summer evening he scooped water from his rain barrel with a pail, then walked along the narrow paths between his beds. He would then dip a metal can, drilled with holes, into the pail, lift it out and gently shower his plants. I watched our neighbours tend their gardens and wished that my father would also organize his plants in tidy rows and water them with a rubber hose that sent an arc of spray high into the air.

Compared to our neighbours, my parents harvested crops that were not only exotic, but downright strange. It was just one more thing that made us different. I hated it when neighbours inquired about the things my father planted. Or when the lady next door smiled and said *how different, how interesting* . . . I wanted my father to grow *lo fon* vegetables— things like carrots, radishes, tomatoes and beets. Instead, we harvested bok choy; gai lan; large winter melons that resembled hoary green pumpkins; long, fuzzy melons; and bitter melons, whose warty skin made them look diseased. When we picked our peas, we never shelled them; we ate the pods, the seeds, everything.

All this was nothing compared to the humiliation I experienced at the end of the summer. My parents soaked their last crop of bok choy in a smelly brown salty brine and then hung the drooping vegetables on the backyard clotheslines to dry. Our laundry was on a corner lot, which allowed all the neighbours to see the limp, wrinkled greens draped over the lines. People asked me what they were for, how we cooked them. I cringed. Worst of all were the few adolescent boys in our neighbourhood who would run through our backyard and shake the clotheslines and knock the stringy bok choy to the ground. When my father ran after them cursing, his old legs unable to keep up, the scrawny boys would turn around and laugh, taunting him with cries of *Chinky Chinky Chinaman*. But in the winter, when my mother made soup with pork bones, red dates, carrots and dried bok choy, the kitchen filled with a fragrant steam that reminded me of summer, and the moment I slurped the delicious broth from my spoon, I knew that *lo fon* food could never be this good.

Early in our travels through rural Kaiping, we were driving beside a river at the edge of Cheong Hong See, when I noticed gardens in the ochre-coloured silt of the flats along its banks. I called to the driver of our van and asked him to stop. My relatives exchanged glances with each other, some of them shaking their heads, as I rushed out of the vehicle and hurried down the embankment. Everything was so familiar: narrow paths dividing mounded beds crowded with bok choy, gai lan, snow peas, winter melon and fuzzy melon. I turned to Michael, who had followed me, and said, "These gardens are just like my father's. This is what it was like behind the laundry." But it hadn't occurred to me then, not even while I crouched down and examined that hodgepodge arrangement of gardens, what now seemed so obvious. Each spring, by making those raised beds and planting vegetables, my father was trying to re-create home. And in doing so, he found solace. But as I looked back, his efforts seemed futile. How could anyone duplicate that emerald paradise in this place of long, unforgiving winters, where the growing season lasted at most five months? On that cold November day, as I gazed at Michael's garden, I began to fathom the depth of sorrow my parents must have felt over the loss of home.

It is true what people say: that you need to be away from your homeland to really understand its hold on you. As a child I had wanted so much to fit in. And to a degree I had succeeded. But I knew even then that no matter how hard I tried, complete acceptance was impossible. I was a Chinese girl living in a white world. We were poor, and my father washed other people's clothes for a living. It didn't matter that I was teacher's pet or that I went to Sunday school and memorized verses from the Bible. At some point I would find myself with my nose pressed up against a window watching others. And yet, since the day that propeller airplane touched down on this soil, this country has been my home. What must it have been like for my parents not just to be homesick but to be marginalized decade after decade? I tapped the dark brown soil in our garden with the toe of my boot, feeling how it had hardened with the drop in temperature. In another six months or so, these beds would be sprouting tiny green shoots.

THIRTEEN

I was sitting in the living room with my old red photo album, which I had found on a shelf between two larger albums. I had started filling it in grade nine but had not opened it in years. I flipped through the pages and saw a picture of me standing on my tricycle in the yard behind my father's laundry, another of me in my Brownie uniform, photos of school friends, a photo of Ming Nee shortly after she'd arrived from Hong Kong. On the front page I'd placed a picture of my mother and one of my father, each dressed in a traditional Chinese jacket with a stand-up collar, buttoning below one shoulder and along the side. In between was a photograph of my mother and me, the earliest image I have of myself. I appear to be about two years old. My mother's straight black hair is chin length, cut blunt and combed behind her ears. She is wearing no makeup. The photographer has tinted my lips and cheeks pink, yet I look like a boy with my hair cropped short, my ears exposed. My mother had always been a practical woman, and in the photo, her daughter is dressed in overalls, with a haircut that required a minimum of fuss.

For the first time it occurred to me that this picture was taken while we were still living in Cheong Hong See. I thought about that junky store and the primitive house in Ning Kai Lee, where my father and his siblings had grown up. I thought about my father's laundry in Acton, where our first soft chair had been a neighbour's discard. And here I was, inside a renovated stone house from the nineteenth century sitting in a comfortable, plush armchair. I looked at the Indian carpet on my floor, the water colours and the pastels on my walls, my collection of glass vases in the bay window. The poverty of my past felt so far away, and yet so close.

I stared for a while at the photograph of my mother and started to think about another one of her I'd seen years before: a small, black-and-white close-up, taken when she was probably in her early twenties. Her hair was black, past her shoulders and parted at the side. Her hands were clasped together and held against her cheek, her head slightly tilted. But despite what the villager in Ning Kai Lee had said, my mother was not beautiful, given her prominent overbite and weak chin. And yet she possessed a compelling face with well-defined cheekbones and a broad forehead. Her dark, coquettish eyes stared directly at the camera. I thought about the young woman in that photograph—her almost flirtatious expression—and wondered if that was the person Jook had recalled for me, the woman who *chased* her father. I had seen another picture of my mother in her twenties, taken in Nanking, where she was going to school. Dressed in dark trousers and a traditional, quilted Chinese jacket, she stood in what appeared to be newly fallen snow. Her arms looked stiff, her shoulders hunched up against the cold. But in this picture, I could not make out her face. These were the only two pictures I had ever seen of my mother as a young woman. As a child I was fascinated with them, I suppose in the way that all children are curious about who their parents were before they'd had children. But because the land of my mother's youth was so far away and so unlike Canada, my fascination was even more accentuated. I often think of those photographs, but I haven't seen either for many years. They were probably lost during one of our moves, or my mother may have tossed them out in anger after my father's death.

My mother first met my father in 1930, when he hired her to teach in his village. The young woman I remembered in those photographs would not have looked much different than the person my father met. She was unlike anyone who had ever lived in, or possibly even visited, Ning Kai Lee. With her education and big city background, she bestowed status on this tiny, impoverished village. When my father first met my mother, he would have been a man of thirty-eight, back from the Gold Mountain, a man in his prime and with considerable status himself. In such circumstances, a prize catch.

The eventual marriage between a woman from an elevated background and an eloquent Gold Mountain guest, who spoke with authority about Confucius and Mencius, China's two greatest philosophers, was for the local villagers whom I met the stuff of fairy tales. As I had listened to their reminiscences, I had been amused by and skeptical of their stories, the mythology that had grown up around my parents, amazed that even though they had not lived in the village for almost sixty years, people knew who they were. But my mother, a beautiful woman? It was hard not to smile. What would these people have told me next? That she walked on water? Sitting in my living room with my old photo album on my lap, I became ashamed of my suspicions. These villagers had seemed to be good people with a genuine interest in me and a fondness for my family. On the other hand, we must have seemed like millionaires returning from El Dorado, arriving in hired vans, hosting banquets, giving away money; perhaps they were just eager to please us.

Until very recently I had never really thought about the "mathematics" of my parents' situation. After my mother left her teaching post in Ning Kai Lee, she would not see my father for about fifteen years and only after the death of his first wife. When she met him again after that long absence, it was to become his second wife. Was it possible that the man she decided to marry was no longer the man who had hired her to teach in the village school? She would have remembered someone still relatively youthful and upright, with a full head of black hair. When he returned to China in 1947, his new passport photograph showed a balding man with a few lingering wisps of hair, and he would have been slightly bent from all the years of labour in the hand laundries. What did my mother think when she set eyes on this man whom she had not seen in a decade and a half but with whom she had chosen to spend the rest of her life? Was she focused only on the future, seeing my father as a means to provide for her and her daughter? Many times she said to me, "I had no choice but to marry your father. But if I hadn't married him, I wouldn't have you and you are my *thlem, gwon,* my heart and my liver." My mother always smiled when she said this, but her words never made me happy.

My mother taught in my father's village for only two or three years. She left because her *thoh* had convinced Big Uncle to send her to Nanking. There she would study silkworm culture and enter an apprenticeship. When she was finished, he would set her up in business and she would finally become financially independent. My mother made it clear to me that she had left the village of Ning Kai Lee not to teach somewhere else or to get married, but to go to school. And not just anywhere; Nanking was the capital of China under the Kuomintang government, a cultured and historic city, still surrounded by massive stone walls, with the Yangtze River to the west and the Purple Mountain to the east, a place of architectural splendours: royal palaces, majestic imperial tombs and grand museums. That someone who had taught in their lowly village had left to "learn from books" in the city of Nanking so dazzled the inhabitants of my father's village that it became a piece of local lore they would never forget.

Growing up in a country where everyone attended school and where I had always assumed I would attend university, I never fully appreciated the significance of my mother's schooling. She carried the memory of those years like a badge of honour. Throughout my childhood I met women who were about the same age as my mother, many of whom came from small farming villages in the south of China. Most of them were illiterate, and they treated my mother with a certain deference. They were impressed not just because my mother could read and write, but because she could read and write so well. No wonder she reminded me, when I was entering university, that she too had gone on to higher education and in no less a place than the city of Nanking.

The year before I started university, I showed my mother a brochure with a picture of the campus I hoped to attend. We were sitting at the kitchen table, only a few feet from the barrel-shaped washing machine. My father was in the adjoining room, finishing up the week's ironing. My mother turned to me and smiled. "Your school looks very nice," she said. "It's too bad that you will never see Nanking, where I was a student. It was a magnificent city with lovely gardens for strolling. The roses and peonies were like none I have seen since. My favourite place though, was Sai Woo, West Lake, in the city of Hangzhou. The lake is in the middle of the city, with hills in the distance. I used to watch the light change on the water, depending on where the sun was in the sky. I walked along those shores many times. It's one of China's most famous sites. I've seen lots of China—Nanking, Shanghai, Canton, the gardens in Suzhou. Not like your father—never been anywhere except his little village. Only passing through cities like Hong Kong and Canton."

"One day when I have lots of money, I will take you back to China," I said in response to her yearning.

My mother's mood suddenly changed. "Don't think about going anywhere," she said sternly. "Just think about school and working hard. Save your money."

She folded my university brochure and handed it back to me. I then placed my red photo album in front of her. I'd added some recent pictures of high school friends and wanted to show them to her. As she turned the pages she said that she too had once kept an album with photographs of her schoolmates in Nanking. She told me about a girl with whom she'd become close and how they'd vowed they would always be friends, her voice choking with regret and sadness. My mother hesitated for a moment and said, "I wasn't always like this, the way I am here. Useless, depending on others to help me. People used to come and ask for my advice, for me to help them. I know you don't believe it."

"Don't worry," I said. "I'll look after you."

As it turned out she never completed her studies in Nanking. Everything had started out with such promise. My mother was a good student; she was popular with the teachers. If it hadn't been for the Japanese, she would say, those hateful Japanese. Because of them her ambitions had turned to ashes.

After capturing Peking in July of 1937, the Japanese started a series of air raids on Shanghai and Nanking. The residents of these cities were ordered to build bomb shelters and to paint the red roofs and white walls of their houses black. The Japanese bombed everything: factories, government buildings, schools, even hospitals. The streets were filled with rubble. Whenever the sirens screamed their warnings, my mother would start to tremble. People would flee the streets, searching for safety. That summer in Nanking was so hot and humid, it was like living in a furnace, she told me. And the Japanese only made it worse.

Big Uncle and her *thoh* sent a telegram, telling her to leave as soon as possible. But she would have left anyway. The bombing raids were becoming more frequent, and she was afraid of being trapped in Nanking. Everywhere around her people were departing in droves; she had to escape while she still could.

The night before my mother fled Nanking, she sewed a secret cloth pouch inside her underpants. The next morning, she packed only a small bag with personal belongings and tucked her money into the pouch next to her belly. Even with a ticket already in hand when she went to the station, it was almost impossible to board the train. People were pushing, shoving, shouting, eyes wide with desperation. Their faces were dripping with sweat from the searing heat. The air had a sour odour that my mother had never encountered before, and she asked herself if this was the smell of fear. As she elbowed her way through the clamouring mob, the press of bodies was so close, she nearly suffocated. But she somehow fought her way onto the train. When she found her seat she was panting, and her clothes were damp against her skin. She heard stories about people climbing on top of the cars and of people tying themselves underneath the train, so desperate to leave the city they were willing to risk death. Some people, especially the poor, had no recourse; they had to remain. Others, who had the means to leave, decided to stay. *Why?* my mother would ask. *To see what might happen?* As far as she was concerned, they were even more foolish than the ones who tied themselves to the bottom of the train.

My mother made it to Shanghai just in time to catch the last boat south to Canton. A few days later Japanese soldiers would invade Shanghai and then march on to ravage Nanking. She had left her album of class photos in Nanking and would never see her best friend again. She was lucky just to get out alive, she told me. Her gratitude would quickly evaporate, however. In the next breath, she would say how unlucky she was to have survived the war, to have witnessed the atrocities that she would eventually see.

Exhausted and relieved, my mother arrived at Big Uncle's mansion in Canton late in the night, after everyone had gone to sleep. One of the servants took her to her old room. The next morning, her *thoh* wept when she saw her and told her she loved her more than anyone else in the world, even more than her own children. With the Japanese now so far away, my mother could finally feel safe.

In her excitement she did not immediately notice the change in her *thoh*. But as my mother looked across the breakfast table, she saw a wraith, a shell of the radiant woman she had left behind a few years before. She stared at her beloved *thoh* and remembered that the previous night, she had heard a raw and incessant cough that seemed to come from the floor above. But she had been bone-tired, and the sound had been muffled by the thick walls of Big Uncle's mansion. In the morning, her worst fears were confirmed.

Throughout my childhood, the disease *fuh loh* was spoken of in hushed, secretive tones. It had a dreaded mystery about it, like leprosy in the Bible, and if you spoke its name too loudly, you might give it life. People who were not ill, but tested positive for the disease, were stranded in China, not allowed to immigrate. My mother once told me about a distant cousin who had been betrothed and, in spite of being healthy, had tested positive for the illness. When the prospective groom's family found out, the marriage was cancelled. The girl was crushed and wept for weeks. *Fuh loh* could ruin your chances at happiness. What did it matter, my mother asked, that this sad girl was born in Canada, well-educated and from a wealthy family? When she finally married in her late thirties, people whispered that it was only because of her father's money. Why else would someone take "tainted goods"?

Fuh loh was tuberculosis, and my mother's *thoh* was very sick with it. Not long after my mother's return to Canton, her *thoh* died.

My mother closed my photo album and picked up a skein of wool from a basket on the floor. She loosened the skein, fitted it over the back of a chair and started to coil the yarn into balls for knitting. When I picked up another skein to fit over another chair, she asked if I had finished my homework. *Yes, yes,* I answered, bristling with impatience over what I felt to be excessive concern. My father was still at the ironing table, now bent over his abacus, tallying the cost of laundry supplies. I could hear the gentle clicking of beads as he slid them up and down on the rungs.

"My *thoh* was a lucky woman, even though she died in her thirties," my mother said to me. My photo album was still triggering memories, ones that I had heard many times before. "She died before the hateful Japanese invaded. She never knew anything but comfort and wealth. Not like me, always unlucky. Born under the wrong signs. It doesn't matter how smart you are or how hard you work. The things I've seen . . . Life was never the same without my *thoh.* When Big Uncle brought her back to the family home as his bride, I was three or four years old. I was six when my own mother died. So you see, it was really my *thoh* who raised me and Little Aunt. And after she died my brother became very cold. I knew I wasn't wanted. But it wasn't all my brother's fault. It was because of Foy Hoo"—*fat woman.*

"You never liked Foy Hoo, did you?" I said.

"Nobody liked Foy Hoo," answered my mother without missing a beat. "She had designs on my brother as soon as she started working for him. She was just a servant girl, no one special. You wouldn't think a man who'd passed the Imperial Examinations could be so easily manipulated, would you? Foy Hoo tried to make things look accidental. Running into my brother in the hall, those tight dresses she wore. But I saw through her. That's why she didn't like me. She knew my *thoh* was dying. She was such a schemer. I saw those secret glances between my brother and her. I once caught them together in an embrace, but they didn't see me. I never told my *thoh*; I didn't have to. Even though she was sick, she knew what was happening.

"Once she walked into the kitchen and saw Foy Hoo sitting at the table, sharing tea with my brother. The two of them were laughing and talking, their heads close together, fingertips touching. My *thoh* was so angry that she picked up a pair of chopsticks and hurled them, knocking over a cup. That woman got up right away and fetched a cloth to mop up the spill. 'Look at her,' my *thoh* said, 'instincts like a low-class servant.' A low-class servant, that's what my *thoh* called her."

My mother finished coiling her skein into a ball and threw it in a basket with the others before loosening another one. I was taken aback at the force of her toss. After all these years, she was still angry with her brother for his betrayal.

"You couldn't fool my *thoh*. She saw the look that woman exchanged with her husband. And Big Uncle pretending he was baffled by his wife's anger. He was just having a cup of tea. What was wrong with that? But my *thoh* knew better. She saw through that Foy Hoo.

"My *thoh* turned out to be right. Not long after she died, Big Uncle took Foy Hoo as a wife. How could he so soon after his first wife's death? *Tseee!* I was more faithful to her memory than he. Can you imagine, I cared more than her husband? And Foy Hoo, that lifeless woman, a mere servant in the house! Unlike my *thoh*, smart and educated. To be replaced by a servant girl. Foy Hoo never liked me, but I didn't care. It was still somewhere to live."

Or so my mother had thought. Less than a year after her *thoh's* death, in October of 1938, the Japanese marched into Canton and occupied the city. She told me that everyone fled Big Uncle's house, and that's when my mother realized that the safest place for her to be was back with her husband, that very no-good man. He lived in the countryside, away from the city.

My mother picked up her knitting needles and started to cast on stitches for a sweater. She said nothing more. I could tell from the way she was concentrating on her hands without ever looking up that her thoughts were still in the past.

FOURTEEN

In 1992 my mother turned eighty. For several years, she'd been living with Michael, our two daughters and me in our Toronto home. After my father's death, she'd been with Doon and his family in a small Ontario city, where he operated a Chinese restaurant. They all lived in the apartment above it, and every day my mother would help out in the restaurant kitchen and dining room. My brother relied on her to scrape the dirty dishes, fill the sugar dispensers, chop vegetables, cook the rice, tidy the tables after the customers left. Even though she was getting too old to be working so much, she left the restaurant with mixed emotions, for there she had maintained a sense of purpose. She'd had no specific role, but she'd been willing to fill the invisible spaces, the gaps between jobs so necessary to make a restaurant run smoothly. But after her doctor diagnosed her with breast cancer, she moved in with us.

She did not smile on the day she left the restaurant and said only a few words during the hour's drive with us to

Toronto. It pained her greatly to know that her days of help-ing out with my brother's business were over.

I knew that at this stage of my mother's life, she belonged in my home, yet I was not without reservations. I was a duti-ful daughter who advocated without hesitation on her behalf, and yet my mother and I did not have an easy relationship. Since my father's death, I'd developed an irrational anger toward her. I'd managed to keep it suppressed, but on rare occasions it would find an opening and unleash itself on her, usually over something petty like the purchase of cheap, sugary cereal for my young daughters, or more ugly plastic dishes, which she had found on sale and which I had neither wanted or needed. My bursts of temper left me feeling ashamed and unkind.

I helped my mother up the stairs to her new bedroom, which was near the washroom. We had bought a new mat-tress for her single bed, and Michael had painted and wall-papered the room for her. I told her I'd do all the cooking and her laundry, that she would be comfortable and had nothing to worry about. She patted me on the arm and said in a small, flat voice, "I know, I know. You take care of every-thing." She then added that she was waiting to die.

I thought that perhaps this had to do with her diagnosis, but with time her mood improved very little, even after the success of her surgery and radiation treatment. She spent her days alone, watching Chinese videos and reading the Chinese newspaper while the rest of us were either at work or at school. I was the only person in the house who spoke Chinese and who was able to converse with her, though I knew how badly my mother wanted to talk with her granddaughters. Every so often they would sit with her in her room, holding her hand and watching Chinese television. But they were adolescents, more interested in their peers than an old woman with whom they could not communicate. We lived in a bright, spacious home on a tree-lined street. But we were far from Chinatown and had no Chinese neighbours. It was in me that she would confide, telling me all her fears.

During the entire time that my mother lived with us, she never mentioned my father. Yet I knew she thought about him. The image of her in a state of near-collapse at his funeral, how she'd had to be helped out of the chapel after his service, her face contorted with pain, distraught with grief, had remained vivid in my memory after all these years.

I arrived home from work, and the moment I closed the front door, my mother called from the second floor, telling me to come quick. She'd been living with us for just over a year. I rushed up the stairs and found her sitting on the edge of her bed, wringing her hands in her lap, her forehead creased with worry lines. I knew she'd been watching the clock for my return. At moments like these, I felt heartsick about the days she spent alone in my house.

She patted the spot beside her, indicating that I should sit down. She pursed her lips together in a way that told me she was about to announce something important. She straightened her back and took a deep breath. Whatever she was about to impart had occupied her mind for a long time. And however minor it might seem to me, this concern would have mushroomed into something monumental.

We were the only people in the house, but she still held her hand to the side of her mouth and whispered that I had to get rid of the cleaning lady. She said that the cleaning lady was a thief and had stolen her underwear. I was shocked, but I also had difficulty suppressing a smile. My cleaning lady weighed at least twice as much as my mother and stood at least a head taller. At best she would have been able to fit one leg into my mother's underpants, even if she'd wanted to steal them. When I stood up and opened her drawer and showed her the missing items, my mother quickly retorted that the cleaning lady had put them back because she knew I was coming home. No matter how much I argued, I could not persuade her that the cleaning lady was not a thief.

"You are too trusting. Your life has been too easy. But I know how a devious mind works," my mother insisted. "Can't you see? The lady doesn't want them for herself. She wants to sell them." Now it was really hard not to laugh. When my mother saw that I was unconvinced, she accused me of siding with the cleaning lady against her. I was ready to point out that her underwear was full of holes, that the cleaning lady would be more likely to use them for rags, when I thought better of it and decided to try another tactic. I said that if the cleaning lady wanted to steal her belongings, she would have taken the new pairs, the ones I'd bought years before, still unused and wrapped in tissue paper, the ones being saved for *good*.

"Do you think I'm stupid? Of course I know that's what she really wanted. *Tsk!*" My mother clucked her tongue and shook her head in exasperation, much in the way that an adult would at an uncomprehending child. "She could have made lots of money if she'd sold my brand-new things. But I saw through her and put them where she can't find them. That's why she took the ones I wear every day. But she's so sneaky she put them back just before you came home."

Finally, I gave up and just told her it was a good thing the undergarments were returned. I said not to worry because, even if all her clothing went missing, I had so much money I'd be able to buy her everything she needed.

My mother gave a sigh of relief. "Good thing you make so much money," she said. "I'm so glad you have such a good job." She hesitated for a moment; then her tone became stern. "Don't ever quit your job. Lots of people want a good job like yours and would steal it if you left." There was that word again. Nevertheless, I was quite pleased with myself for stumbling onto this clever diversion.

Then she suddenly perked up. She thrust her head forward, about to begin a mission. "Have you paid off your mortgage yet?" she demanded, wagging a finger. "That's what's most important. Forget nice clothes and holidays. What's most important is good food and paying off your mortgage. Chinese people don't like owing money and paying interest. Not like *lo fons, chargee* this, *chargee* that." It served me right, bragging about imaginary wealth, even if it was just to put her at ease. When I tried to change the topic of conversation again, she became stubborn and fixated on whether I still had a mortgage. Finally,

I capitulated and told her what she wanted to hear. I mumbled under my breath and said that we had paid off our house. A broad, satisfied grin broke across her face.

"Thank god. Now I can die without worry. And thank goodness you married a good *lo fon*. I suppose every group has good and bad. You could have just as easily married a bad Chinese, someone who smokes and gambles. You're lucky. Michael looks after his family, and he knows how to fix everything, saves a lot of money. And he's not like some people, *chargee* this, *chargee* that."

All concerns about the cleaning lady had vanished, at least for now. I was happy to end our conversation with the topic of thrift and my *marvellous* husband. Michael chuckled whenever he heard reports of my mother's boasting. She had been reluctant to accept him when we first met. While we were still an unmarried couple, she continued to tell me about "good" Chinese boys who were looking for a wife, with whom Matchmaker Auntie would be more than happy to organize a meeting. I never took my mother's suggestions seriously. She grew frustrated with my dismissive attitude, and as a final resort she told me it wouldn't *hurt* to meet one of these boys. It wasn't as if it was going to cost anything. Matchmaking services were always paid for by the groom, she pointed out. But now she couldn't stop extolling Michael's virtues, to the point of fabrication. She had decided in her own mind that her son-in-law was a saver, someone who used only cash. Credit cards, as far as she was concerned, were for less worthy and less responsible *lo fons*. Chinese people never touched them. According to my mother.

A few days after the cleaning lady incident, she went for a walk after supper and became lost. Michael hopped on his bicycle and searched out our neighbourhood. Once he found her, he raced home and got in the car. It was a warm summer evening, so I was not concerned with her falling or catching a chill. We both knew she walked so slowly that she would not be far from where he had originally found her. When she arrived home she was unaware that she had gone for a walk and thought her kind son-in-law had taken her for a summer evening's drive.

Another night, not long afterwards, my family was seated around the kitchen table. I'd made spaghetti with meat sauce for dinner that night, one of my mother's favourite meals, since after Chinese, Italian was her preferred cuisine. Right up until her death, she continued to love food and maintained a good appetite. We had almost finished eating, when my mother asked me if I had ever been to Miami. I shook my head, and she informed me that she had been many times. I stared at her, my fork held in mid-air. While she was living with Doon, she and a girlfriend had taken a bus tour of Los Angeles and San Francisco. Once, she had even been to New York City with Ming Nee. But other than these two trips, she had travelled very little since leaving China. She had certainly never even been close to Florida.

My mother ignored my reaction and said that it was easy to get to beautiful Miami. Dumbfounded, I asked her, "How?"

"There's a bridge from Hong Kong to Miami," my mother said. "You can walk across it. Very easy."

I almost choked on my pasta. I put down my fork, barely able to keep a straight face, and said, "That's not possible. There's no bridge connecting the two cities."

My mother turned her head in my direction, her eyes steady with confidence. "You don't know everything. I'm the one who should know. I walked across that bridge." I let the conversation drop, and my mother requested a second helping. I asked one of my daughters to get up and replenish her grandmother's plate.

Every night our dinner table had two simultaneous conversations, one in Chinese between me and my mother and one in English for everyone else. There were times when I was expected to participate in both simultaneously, and I often lost track. But that night Michael and our daughters had stopped talking, suddenly drawn into an exchange they could not comprehend. My husband asked, "What's your mother so worked up about?' When I told my family, they smiled. But Michael's eyes looked worried.

My daughter set the refilled plate in front of her grandmother and started to cut the pasta into shorter lengths. Before sitting down she gave her grandmother a quick hug. As I watched my mother and my daughter, I could no longer deny that my mother's mind had become like a boat without moorings. The moment a conversation was finished, we could begin the same one again, and for her it was as if nothing had been said before. I remembered noticing that she could read the same article in a newspaper several times repeatedly without seeming to realize it. My amusement vanished, and I suddenly felt short of breath. The day before I had returned home and found a tap left running. Tomorrow, it might a pot left boiling on the stove.

The Chinese home for the aged in downtown Toronto had a space available for my mother. It was a good fit. The staff spoke a number of Chinese dialects, and they served only Chinese food. Each floor had a communal living room with comfortable chairs and a television. I could borrow a wheelchair and easily take her to Chinatown nearby for dinner or dim sum lunch. For the first year or so she responded well to her new surroundings. Her mind was still generally able to navigate between her past and her present. But there was no denying that the world in which she lived was fading from her consciousness. She constantly talked about her childhood. Little things triggered her memories: a favourite food, a flower in a bouquet, an item of clothing. She told me again and again about going to Sunday school with her younger sister in Taishan, where they grew up. She told me again how the missionaries there had taught her to knit, embroider and crochet. She would sing in Chinese, "Jesus Loves Me" and "Hark! the Herald Angels Sing," her voice tuneful and sweet. But whenever she asked me, "Do you want to know the real reason I went to Sunday school?" I knew her reminiscences were about to end. My mother would beckon me to come closer. She would chuckle and whisper to me as if I were a fellow conspirator. "I went to Sunday school not because I believed. Although there's nothing wrong with believing. My little sister and I went because the missionaries gave us biscuits and cakes to eat, free. Lots of children believed for the same reason." After divulging this little secret, she always giggled and then disappeared once again into her childhood.

A few months after my mother moved to the nursing home, I visited her with a bag of fresh lychees. I found her in the communal living room, watching television. I peeled several of the fruit and put them on a plate I'd taken from her room. She was watching a war movie. On the screen terrified people were screaming and fleeing from random explosions. She pointed to the scene and said, "That's what it was like. The bombs. They fell out of the sky, and you never knew where they would land. Somehow I managed to miss them, and I always managed to find safety for my daughter and me. I used to see children left by the side of road. They were crying and dirty, deserted by their parents. But I could never do that. I would rather die first."

My mother once again reminded me how lucky I was, not to know any of the misfortune she had known. And when she asked me if I knew that she was sixteen when she was married, she didn't wait for an answer. She proceeded once more to tell me the story of her terrible first marriage. Again, I half-listened. I had heard her account before, and without any help could probably repeat it, word for word.

I had known for a long time that after the death of her *thob*, sometime around the Japanese invasion of Canton, my mother had returned to her first husband. Big Uncle's fortunes had fallen, and there was the matter of his marriage to Foo Hoy, Fat Lady, the woman my mother never liked. There must also have been a general sense of chaos in the city and an "every man for himself" sort of mentality. She felt her only choice was to seek refuge with this man whom she despised, to whom she was still married.

I thought I knew this story inside out. But this time as I listened, it occurred to me that she could have gone back to her father. Her mother had died when she was a child, but surely her own father would have given her a home. When I interrupted and asked, she said, "My father was dead. He had died even before I was married, when I was twelve or thirteen. I'm not sure anymore. It was a long time ago. My father was murdered."

Murdered?

My mother picked up one of the lychees and ate it, then put the pit on the plate. She looked at me and shook her head. "My father was a very sociable person. He loved people. That's why he was such a good doctor. After a house call on that particular day, instead of coming straight home, he went to a teahouse to chat with some friends. Some soldiers saw him go in. My sister and I, when we saw soldiers roaming the streets we were afraid. There were always stories about how they often didn't get paid, sometimes not even fed. So they stole to survive. When they saw my father's doctor's bag, they must have thought it was full of money. Anyway, when he came out, they followed him and they clubbed him to death. They were probably angry that he didn't have any money, at least not what they expected. I became an orphan at an early age. Now do you see why my *thoh* was so important to me? She was really the only mother I ever had. That's why her death was so terrible. I wasn't lucky like you, living in Canada with a mother who worries about you. In another few years I won't be here, and then you'll see. You don't know how lucky you are to have a mother who worries about you. After my *thoh* died, nobody worried about me. What else could I do but return to that very no-good man?"

I stared back at her, my mouth a gaping hole. *Murdered!* Her tone was so casual; she could just as easily have been talking about the weather. I wrapped my arm around her shoulder. Reeling from this revelation about my grandfather whom I had never met, his bloody, violent death, I was ashamed that I was a middle-aged woman before I had even asked how he had died. Sitting beside my mother, I felt a world apart from her, to think that my parents had spent their childhoods in a place where an event as terrible as her father's murder was not unusual.

I walked my mother to her table in the dining room and waited for her to sit down. The food at this home was exceptional. Everything was cooked from scratch, and the residents routinely ate fresh seafood. Every evening meal started with a long-simmered soup. I bent over and kissed her goodbye.

I decided to walk the several blocks north before catching the streetcar. The chestnut trees were covered with cone-shaped clusters of white blossoms. Front yard gardens were sprouting bok choy, gai lan and other Chinese greens. I passed a few people on this quiet, residential street. Most people were already home from work, and I caught the occasional whiff of garlic frying in oil. The streetcar was full when I got on. I pushed my way to the back, where there was space to stand, annoyed that people were crowding the front and blocking the entrance.

My mother had lived in Canada for more than forty years, yet she continued to be burdened by her past, still suspicious of life in the Gold Mountain. If my family left for a holiday, I had faith that when we returned, our home would still be standing and our furniture would be undisturbed. My irritations felt petty; my decisions felt almost frivolous: what university to attend, where to vacation, which house to buy, what to serve at a particular dinner party, what outfit to wear. When I arrived home, Michael and I would eat last night's leftovers on matching dishes. After dinner I would load the dirty dishes inside my fancy dishwasher. I would spend the rest of the evening relaxing, perhaps watching the news on TV before going to bed. My husband and I both had secure jobs; the girls were both at university. What had I done in my past life to deserve living on my safe, tidy planet?

I should be grateful. I was grateful. But resentment lurked under my skin. I hated it when she told me how lucky I was to have a mother who worried about me. On some level I was not the good Chinese daughter that she wanted. I was too Western, too independent. My devotion to her was no match for hers to me. My mother never missed an opportunity to warn me how sorry I'd be once she was gone. And how right she has turned out to be.

In the last year of my mother's life, her delusions became steadily worse and more frequent. Many times I would arrive in her room and find her alone, talking or singing songs with an imaginary friend from her youth. Often, it was her younger sister. A few months before she died, my mother had to be hospitalized for some internal bleeding. When I entered her hospital room, a young, black nurse was sitting beside her and holding her hand. My mother was having a one-sided conversation with her in Chinese. The woman nodded and smiled. As soon as my mother saw me, she told me to hurry over. She introduced me to her new friend, giving her a Chinese name. She told me that the "young girl" was from a neighbouring village and had walked a long way just to visit her. I was pleased to see my mother in this rare, buoyant mood, but at the same time my heart sank. Though she still recognized me and knew my name, I felt her slipping away.

Michael and I took our daughters to visit their grandmother in the nursing home on a Saturday. Ming Nee saw her on Sunday. The following afternoon the nursing home called me to let me know that she had died. My mother was eighty-eight years old. She had recently seen the people who meant the most to her. It was her time to go. She felt no need to give us warning.

At her funeral we burned spirit money, paper spirit clothing and furniture, so she would not be without in her afterlife.

We burned incense so that her spirit would be at peace. And before the closing of the coffin, each of her children, along with other family members, tucked a blanket around her, ensuring her warmth and comfort. With my mother we had the satisfaction of saying goodbye.

FIFTEEN

Even if my mother's *thoh* had lived, with Big Uncle's fortunes in decline, she could not have offered refuge from the Japanese in an occupied city. And so my mother returned to the countryside and appealed for sanctuary to a man she hated, a man she had had little to do with for almost ten years. It is hard for me to imagine a more humbling situation than the one my mother faced. In June 1942, while she was living with this man, she gave birth to my half-sister Ming Nee. This period of relative security with her first husband was brief, for not long after the birth, my mother and her baby had to escape from the invading Japanese soldiers. I cannot imagine how terrible life with that very no-good man must have been to make her leave during such a dangerous time. She never explained to me why she chose to be on her own. I can only guess.

She and her baby daughter fled toward Hong Kong. For a while she found work in a telegraph office, interpreting incoming Morse code messages that warned of the Japanese advance. From listening to my mother, it seemed that there were periods of relative safety, but then she might awaken to find the Japanese invaders practically at her doorstep. She talked about bombs raining down from the sky. If she ran too fast or too slow, she risked being blown to shreds. During her periods of flight, she found safety in caves and abandoned buildings. She was so starved, she dug roots out of the ground to eat. While she was in hiding, she saw people herded together and bayoneted. She saw a soldier slice open a pregnant woman. She shielded her daughter's eyes from these acts of horror, which left her mouth dry and her chest pounding, her body weak from fear and hunger. She watched and prayed that they would not be found. She lived in constant worry that her daughter might inadvertently cry out, but she never did. Even though Ming Nee was just a little over the age of two, she understood that their lives depended on being silent, that a tiny peep could result in death.

My mother never forgave the Japanese. We had some distant relatives in Toronto who were Canadian-born Chinese and who rented the second floor of their house to a Japanese family, also Canadian-born. On a few occasions when we visited, we crossed paths with members of this family, and my mother always turned away, her lips clamped shut, her anger locked inside. It didn't matter that these people had had nothing to do with the Japanese soldiers who invaded China. As far as she was concerned, the bombs that fell on Hiroshima and Nagasaki were justified. Without them the Japanese would have permanently occupied and brutalized China. While I was single, she admonished me never to marry a Japanese man. She threatened never to speak to me again if I disobeyed her.

Her flight from the Japanese continued without destination. My mother had hoped to find refuge in Hong Kong with her older sister and her family. But once the Japanese occupied the city, they closed the borders and did not allow people from the Mainland to enter. My guess is that she arrived in Hong Kong only after the Japanese had been defeated. I don't know how long she stayed with her older sister and her family. It may only have been a few months, yet that period of her life always seemed charmed. After living with danger for so long, she finally felt safe. And she was with people who loved her.

According to my mother, of the three sisters in her family, the oldest was the most beautiful and the youngest was the most gentle. In her next breath, she would proclaim without embarrassment that she, the middle one, was the most clever. She bragged that she was the smartest one in school and that she always learned new things faster than her younger sister. Nonetheless, the oldest, Family Beauty, enjoyed the most good fortune. Because of her looks she had attracted a husband who was not only a rich businessman from Hong Kong, but also a man with a kind and generous disposition. Even with their wealth and position, they and their five children had barely survived the Japanese occupation. It was in their home that my mother and her daughter found refuge after the war.

Although my mother felt at the mercy of Big Uncle's goodwill, her *thoh* had made a place for her in his family. After Big Uncle married Foo Hoy, things changed, little by little, for the worse. "Oh, Foo Hoy had a nice tongue," my mother said. "Foo Hoy said all the right things. But she never liked me. And with the Japanese, everything was hard and food was scarce. But every once in a while there would be something good to eat, maybe somebody managed to find and catch a stray chicken. You know what Foo Hoy would do? She'd wait until I was out of the house before she'd cook it. As if I couldn't tell. As if the food had no smell. What did she think I was? A fool? But at my sister's house, they shared everything. No matter how little they had."

The few years between the birth of Ming Nee and my mother's marriage to my father are vague. But at some point, in spite of the friction between my mother and Foo Hoy, Big Uncle must have encouraged her to return to his home in Canton. Her arrival created an untenable situation for him, placing him uncomfortably between his wife and a favourite sister. But my mother was unable to empathize with her brother's dilemma, as she never forgave him for his second marriage. I'm only beginning to perceive the love my uncle must have felt for his sister, though, and the weight of his responsibility as head of the family.

Mo tin mo meung, no money, no life, was a mantra that my mother repeated to me many times while I was growing up. So many of her decisions were underpinned by this single belief. Indeed, after the war was over, my mother found herself with no money and no means of support. People were beginning to rebuild their lives, and even though she could rely on relatives for food and housing, she knew that with a young daughter who would have to go to school, she needed money that neither Big Uncle nor Family Beauty could any longer afford. Sometime after returning to Canton, she found out, by coincidence or by her own inquiries, that my father had been stranded in Canada for the entire war and that his wife had died, leaving his children essentially orphaned. His oldest son, Hing, was married, but with a young family of his own, he was in no position to care for his three growing siblings, Jook, Shing and Doon.

My mother assessed the possibilities. She approached securing a future for herself and her daughter as pragmatically as if it were a business transaction, accepting that this would be a decision without sentiment. I've often wondered, if I had been in the same position, whether I would have been able to act with the same decisiveness. Even though her actions make me wince, at the same time I can't help but admire this woman who took such resolute control of her life.

One day, not long after the war ended, my father received a notice at the laundry that a registered letter was waiting for him at the post office. Knowing my father, he would not have rushed off. Whatever he was doing, whether hanging a load of laundry or ironing a shirt, he would have completed his task. He would also have worried that the letter might be something from the government, telling him he had to leave the country or that he owed money. For my parents, fear of authority was never far away, and my father was only too aware of his lowly status in Canadian society. He told me many times how foreigners occupying one of the concessions in Shanghai had infamously posted a sign outside Huangpu Park that read, "No dogs or Chinese allowed." This, he declared, was just another example of the humiliation the Chinese tolerated at the hands of foreign powers. It wasn't until I was an adult that I discovered this sign had been posted in the 1830s, more than fifty years before my father was born. As far as he was concerned, *lo fon* authorities still had no use for the Chinese.

I can almost see the relief on my father's face that particular day in 1945 when he signed for the registered letter and saw that it wasn't from the government. A registered letter from China might bring bad news, but once he saw my mother's name above the return address, those concerns would have vanished, leaving only curiosity. My father was not an impulsive man, so he would have brought the letter back to his laundry, to the privacy of his home, before opening it. Once the door was closed behind him, would he have opened it right away or did he lay it on the ironing table's smooth, white surface and gaze for many minutes at the airmail envelope with the once-familiar handwriting, handwriting that he would not have seen for almost fifteen years? He could only have guessed what this woman wanted from him. My father would eventually have taken a pair of scissors, carefully snipped a hairline strip along the short end of the envelope, removed and unfolded the onion skin paper and read the rows of characters written in black ink.

When my father travelled to Canada in 1936, he had planned to go back to China in another few years, but in 1937 the Japanese invaded, and then his wife died not long after the outbreak of the war in Europe. My father was stranded in Canada. First Brother Hing, and his teenaged bride of only a few months were now responsible for Hing's three young siblings. Shing, the oldest of the younger children, wrote letters to his father in a script that was clumsy and immature, yet he managed to communicate that food was scarce and that sometimes the money that was sent home was gambled away by First Brother. As my father read these letters from his young son, he must have been overwhelmed by helplessness, his tears smudging the ink.

According to Shing, 1943 was the worst year of the war because of the famine. Several families in the village died. There were rumours of cannibalism. For days on end, he, Jook and Doon ate nothing but a watery gruel made from a few grains of rice. Doon once stole a meal of scraps from a cat. He became so thin that the bones in his shoulders protruded and his skin stretched so tightly over his ribs they looked like ridges on a scrub board. But Shing became bloated, his stomach like a taut balloon, his eyes sunken in a hollow face. Neighbours occasionally took in and fed four-year-old Doon. At age nine, Jook helped out in people's kitchens, and whatever food she managed to scrounge she would share with her brothers. According to my father, Shing had the most difficult time of all his children. He was ten years old and no longer cute like Doon. People looked at Shing and saw only another mouth to feed. Yet he was still a child, not old enough to do a man's work. Shing never forgot Jook's loyalty, and when he came to Canada, he continued to send her money in memory of her kindness.

An older cousin in the village, to whom our father had at one time sent money so that he could complete high school, became alarmed when he saw the three starving children. He gave them a weekly allowance and told my sister not to give the money to First Brother for fear that he might lose it gambling. He instructed the three children to use the cash to buy food and to wait until First Brother and his family had finished eating before cooking for themselves. This cousin kept a tally of the money and told the children that their father could pay him back once the war was over. The cousin is no longer alive and whether my father repaid him or was even told about the money none of my siblings claim to know. My intuition tells me that he never did keep an account, but pretended to, so my family would save face.

When my mother's letter arrived, my father must already have been planning to return to China to reunite with his children. As he looked down one column after another, reading the polite salutations and inquiries about his health, all written in my mother's distinctive hand, he would have become ever more curious as to why she was writing him. As he came to the end of her missive, he would have received his answer. My mother was proposing marriage.

I have always wondered how she couched her proposal. Did she flatter my father? He never expanded on the simple fact that my mother had written and asked him to marry her. My mother never told me about the letter at all—only that his children needed someone to look after them and she needed someone to provide her and her daughter with a future. The union she offered could prove mutually beneficial.

I was perhaps nine or ten when my father told me about the letter. They had just had another terrible quarrel. It was almost as if he was saying to me that he wasn't entirely to blame for her unhappy situation. When he married my mother, he continued, she had concealed the fact that her first husband was still alive and that she was still married to him. My father shook his head and said that discovering this had been a terrible situation for him, a loss of face. I felt sorry for my father, but I was also beginning to appreciate how desperate my mother must have felt, her need to survive trumping any residual shred of pride.

I can only speculate as to whether she at some point after they married informed my father that she was still married or whether her first husband arrived, declared himself and possibly demanded compensation. But my father did sort the matter through, and my mother did, in fact, divorce that very no-good man. When my father finished his story, I didn't know what to say. Throughout my childhood my parents whispered secrets to me about each other. These confidences always started with: *Don't tell your . . . but did you know that . . . .* By confiding in me I felt that my father was staking a territorial claim on my affections, inviting me to look inside a box that held unflattering secrets about my mother—stories my mother would not have wanted me to hear. But of course my father never knew about the things my mother told me about him. I was already aware of her reluctance to come to Canada and that it was not just because of having to leave Ming Nee in Hong Kong.

Not long after my father's return to China in 1947, my mother introduced her new husband to Big Uncle at an expensive restaurant in Canton, where they had a dim sum lunch. I can see my father's ingratiating smile, eager to please this man of high rank. But Big Uncle was not impressed with my father's status as a Gold Mountain guest. Afterwards, when Big Uncle and my mother were alone, he told her that she had made a bad decision, marrying well beneath their family. Her confession to me always ended with *Mo vun fut. I had no choice. I had no choice.*

At these times she just assumed that I had taken her side. But I hated hearing these confessions and wanted to hurl blame at her. *You're the one who asked him to marry you!* And so I became a reluctant receptacle for my parents' mutual contempt. When I looked at them I could feel these secrets, alive inside me, hissing at each other like angry snakes. I wanted to release them and be rid of them. Instead, I carved my heart into deep compartments, a place for each secret, never allowing one to touch the other.

In my child's mind I had always imagined a jubilant reunion. In 1947, when my father's ship from Canada arrived in Hong Kong, my mother and her daughter were there to meet him. I could see my mother and father waving the moment they caught sight of each other, then pushing through the crowds and finally embracing. Together, they took a boat to Kaiping City. From there they hired a sedan chair to my father's village. I pictured my father helping my mother and her daughter into the chair. I saw my father tweaking Ming Nee's round cheek, the three of them laughing and joking all the way back to Ning Kai Lee. I had wanted them to be in love, and in my desperation had created a wistful past full of joy. I now see that after a separation of almost fifteen years, they would more likely have greeted each other and their forthcoming marriage with guarded hopes and wary eyes.

SIXTEEN

Your mother chased my father. As I was leaning into the flower bed in front of our house, cutting dead blossoms off our day lilies, I could have sworn that I heard my sister's hoarse voice. I stood up with the sensation that if I turned around, I would see her standing behind me, a sly grin on her face, her whisperings provocative. There were times when I felt that Jook had sneaked on the plane with us and was now living in my home. For months her words had resonated in my head, rushing over me unbidden while I was occupied with some mundane chore—hanging laundry, raking leaves, weeding the garden.

What could *you* possibly know? How could *you* possibly know the truth? That was how each imaginary conversation with my sister started. You were a child of, what, maybe six, when our father left for Canada *and* you were married within a year after he returned in 1947. You barely knew him. You would have known him and my mother as a couple for only those few short years before he had to leave for Canada again.

Well, *I'm* the one who lived with them in that wretched laundry on the other side of the Pacific. *You* didn't hear the fighting, feel the bitterness, the anger, the loneliness that seeped into every crevice of their lives. *You* don't even know how our father died. I do. *I* was there. *I* was the one who held my quivering mother as we watched his body, draped in a white sheet, being taken away in an ambulance.

Whenever I found myself longing for a moment of grace, of shared happiness in my parents' lives, hoping that perhaps there was some shred of truth in the fairytale I heard back in China, I would hear my mother's voice, mimicking Big Uncle's contempt and disbelief the first time he met my father. "*You married him?* That's what Big Uncle said to me when we were alone. I felt nothing but shame," my mother said. "What could I do? Either marry this small man from Ning Kai Lee or starve. When I was a girl, I had no idea that my life would be so terrible. First that very no-good man, then a man who washed other people's clothes. My father was a doctor and my brother had passed the Imperial Examinations."

It was the middle of August. We'd already booked our plane tickets for China, leaving at the end of September, almost exactly a year since our first trip. But this journey would be different from the one I'd taken with my brothers. Michael and I were going on our own. I wanted time to savour the county my parents had known as young people. I would try to discover more about them and in doing so, dispel the mythology that had grown around them. My parents were decent, hard-working people, whose lives deserved to be honoured in a truthful way, not tainted with fabrications. No one in my Canadian family spoke openly about my father's death. No one ever uttered the word *suicide*. The closest anyone came to that forbidden word was *the way he died*. In fact, he was rarely mentioned. After the funeral we returned to the business of living—of getting up each morning, going to work, making dinner, going to bed—as if he had never been a part of it. This man to whom so many in my family owed their current prosperity had been erased. Our lives in Canada were agreeable and middle-class. We had done our best to bury the shame, anger, guilt, hurt and humiliation that had washed over us after his suicide. But privately, his death still haunted me. This diligent and selfless man, whose life had ended with tragedy, made me uncomfortable. Here it was more than thirty years later. And still, whenever I thought about my father's suicide, something inside my chest would start to constrict. I wanted to open a window; I wanted to feel a rush of clean air; I wanted to take a deep breath and exhale.

In another few weeks, Michael and I would split any perennials that had grown too large, replanting half in the mature bed and the other in a newly dug flower bed. A few days before leaving for China, we would trim them all back. By then our vegetables would have been harvested, some frozen, most given away, and the soil would have been turned over in preparation for next year's planting. My husband would have finished cutting, splitting and stacking firewood for the winter. We would then close up our house, have a last visit with our daughters, son-in-law and granddaughter. We would be gone for six weeks.

PART THREE
Second Journey

The way my mother told it, she, Big Uncle and her *thoh* were the stars in their family story, much of which took place in the mansion in Canton and ended with her marriage to my father. The very no-good man made only a cameo appearance. Little Aunt barely deserved a mention. The impression I had gleaned from my mother's recollections was that only she, of all her siblings, had lived there with Big Uncle and his family. But after chatting with Kung last year and hearing that his mother had also lived in the Canton mansion, I began to question my mother's version of life with Big Uncle and her *thoh*.

Before leaving for China this second time, I visited with Shing, and he told me that when Little Aunt was a teenager, she had won a local beauty contest. I left my brother's house puzzled about why my mother had kept this from me. Little Aunt's victory was no major accomplishment like Big Uncle's passing the Imperial Examinations, but would it not have been the sort of happy memory an older sister would share with her family?

After my father bought that old television, I watched it whenever I had time. My parents hardly watched at all. They had few spare moments, and Chinese programming was not yet available. My mother, however, made an exception when it came to watching beauty pageants. Every year she and I looked forward to Miss World, Miss Universe and Miss America. We tried to guess the winner and often disagreed with the judges' selection of finalists. The year that Miss Thailand was crowned Miss Universe, we were both thrilled that an Asian had won. All my life I had assumed that my mother had enjoyed these shows because they could be appreciated without understanding English. She never told me that her own sister had won a beauty contest. She had acknowledged that Little Aunt was pretty but was always quick to add that people preferred *her* company, found *her* more interesting and easy to talk to.

The dark side of my heart asks what emotions besides love lurked behind my mother's generosity toward her younger sister. Was there envy and resentment? Had she spent her childhood in the shadow of this pretty girl? Once she was living in Gam Sun, were her gifts of money and the carefully chosen pictures of our life in the Gold Mountain intended to remind her sister that she, Yet Lan, was the "lucky" one, living in a land of limitless good fortune? I find it hard not to be impressed that my mother sent money and pictures not just for a few years, but for several decades. And yet that impression is tainted when I consider that she might have done so out of prolonged envy or even just habit. I remember a particular visit with my mother in her nursing home toward the end of her life. I found her looking lost in the chair beside her bed. I put my arm around her; she seemed so vulnerable, like a child who had been crying. She then told me that her little sister had just left. She told me how much she missed her. I smiled. Perhaps in the end love did prevail.

Street hawkers, beggars and hustlers pressed in on us and made the congested sidewalks hard to negotiate. Michael was a magnet in Gong Bei, the border town next to Macau. Kung and Lin kept telling us to ignore the entreaties and not to give money to the beggars, otherwise we'd be swarmed. Only a few moments before, we'd been in Macau with its splendid, seventeenth-century Portuguese colonial architecture. Here in this border town, on the Mainland side, everything was filthy, dilapidated and chaotic. The traffic was worse than in Kaiping. Vehicles were making random U-turns and passing each other from either side; 125CC motorbikes wove between the cars and trucks, occasionally driving up onto the sidewalk and bullying pedestrians out of the way. There were few traffic lights, and crossing intersections was an exercise in bluffing and aggression. I felt safe crossing the road only when we were in the middle of a large crowd. When we arrived at the bus station, some of the frenzy was left behind, but the contrast between this town and Macau struck me still. The sidewalks of black-and-white mosaic tiles in Senado Square were already a waning memory.

For most of the two-hour drive from Gong Bei to the village of Sai Woo, located at the edge of Taishan City, our bus travelled on a four-lane toll highway with almost no traffic. My cousin told the driver to stop outside his village, and from there Kung called a taxi on his cell phone. As the only son in the family, my cousin had inherited the family home in Sai Woo. He'd never lived there as a child because his family had lived in Enping County, where his father had been an architect for the city planning department. All the same, he referred to himself as being from Taishan, and a few years back, he'd demolished the house in Sai Woo and built a new one in its place.

The three-storey, four-bedroom home has all the Western amenities, yet it is still in keeping with the surrounding village. It also has metal bars on the outside doors and windows. In some ways my cousin's house is a modest version of the watch towers built in the 1920s—plain by comparison but nevertheless a proud statement about the prosperity he'd reaped while he was away from home.

Michael realized early on that Kung's invitation to stay at this village house was an opportunity rarely available to Westerners. I too was enthusiastic, but now had another reason to visit with my cousin. I wanted to find out more about Little Aunt. Kung told us that Michael was probably the first *lo fon* to spend the night in his village and, sure enough, several neighbours dropped by minutes after our arrival, primarily, I suspected, to have a look at my husband.

Though larger, Sai Woo was much like Ning Kai Lee, with paths between the houses so narrow that Michael could stand in the middle and touch the walls of the houses on either side. There were more newly constructed houses, but the old ones were made of the same grey brick that I had seen the year before in my ancestral village. During one of our walks, Kung pointed to the decorative tiles along the roof ridges of each house. They were beautifully sculpted and detailed, but where they should have jutted beyond the roof into a graceful upward curve, they were jagged and truncated. At one time each ridge had ended with an ornamental dragon, situated to guard the home against evil spirits. But during the Cultural Revolution, the government had deemed these symbols counter-revolutionary and had exhorted the Red Guards to smash these remnants of China's past superstitious beliefs.

"My family was especially persecuted because of our connection to Big Uncle and because my father had been a civil servant during the Kuomintang era," said Kung. "Even though he was never a member of the Kuomintang, the Communists still classified him an enemy of the people. During the Cultural Revolution, he was publicly paraded and forced to wear a sandwich board, denouncing himself." He went on, bitterly: "Our family suffered a lot because of those connections. You're lucky that your father was able to sponsor you to Canada. Otherwise, you would have been like me, sent into the countryside for re-education. Instead of going to school,

I had to plant rice and look after pigs." My cousin paused and shook his head. "The one who had the worst time was Big Uncle's oldest son. He was stuck in Canton, and during the Revolution, he was forced to scrub latrines and was publicly beaten. He survived terrible humiliation. The government let him live in a single room in the mansion where he grew up, but the rest of the house was occupied by strangers. It was a terrible time for all of us."

My cousin's words reminded me of my nieces and nephews in Kaiping who had also suffered during the Cultural Revolution. My mother had told stories about people being tortured not long after the Communist takeover. There was an aunt whose husband had been a wealthy landowner. The new regime labelled them as enemies of the people and forced them to kneel for days, from sunrise to sundown. They were not allowed to move and were beaten if they did. At the end of each day, when they were permitted to rise and leave for home, they were soaked in their own waste and barely able to walk.

Each morning we woke to the sound of a rooster crowing and to neighbours chatting in the narrow street below. Being located at the edge of Taishan City and only a couple of hours' drive from Macau and Hong Kong, Sai Woo village had not escaped the rapid industrialization in this part of southern China. Kung explained that until ten years before, it had still been a farming village, surrounded by vegetable and rice fields and a large fish pond. The pond had since been filled in and was now grown over with scrub and weeds. The paved village forecourt, which in the past would have been used for drying crops, had been turned into a dumping site for household garbage, construction debris and old chicken coops. Weeds sprouted in the cracks of its broken cement. My cousin complained about the terrible mess that the entrance to his village had become. Most of the land that had been communally farmed by the village was now leased to nearby factories and had been used to build low-rise apartments to house their workers. This ultimately made more money for the villagers than they could earn by raising food. Kung pointed to some deserted plots, which, like the pond, were now thick with weeds and littered with rubble. He said the villagers were still waiting for government permits to allow the construction of even more dormitories.

A few small gardens were growing near the river, and it was apparent that, with these, some villagers were trying to maintain a semblance of their old lifestyle. We'd occasionally see them returning to their homes, carrying empty water buckets dangling from the ends of a yoke after they'd irrigated their plots. Several water buffalo grazed on the river flats, but we saw no trace of the rice fields that at one time would have covered the area. These animals, symbols of China's ancient rural past, looked incongruous against a background of factories, a shopping mall and nightclubs.

My cousin told me that a ridge had once surrounded the village on three sides. Because of this land formation, the village was nicknamed Crab Village. But a few years ago, the

ridge was flattened to make way for new building develop-
ments. I noticed the sandy yellow soil; reshaping this landscape with modern machinery would have been easy, perhaps
too easy. I was secretly pleased that my father's village was
far from any large urban area.

៙

Kung was taking us on a tour of Taishan City, once known
as Little Canton, where our mothers had lived when they
were children. As we walked around its commercial streets,
it was evident that Taishan City had once been a prosperous place. The buildings were the same vintage as the watch
towers we'd visited the year before, with the same odd mix
of foreign architectural influences. We encountered one
street that had been completely restored, the buildings
painted colourful pastels, allowing tourists like me to get a
glimpse of its former glory. Prior to the Japanese invasion
in 1937, this town, and in fact, the entire region, had been
teeming with commercial activity because of its proximity
to Hong Kong and Macau. I could see why my father had
thought it would be possible to live out his days in comfort
in the Four Counties.

On the way to our mothers' childhood home, we stopped
at a scenic park filled with gardens and a network of spring-
fed ponds connected by canals. While we were walking
around the park admiring the grounds, Kung told us that the
ponds and canals had been dug by hand. Not long after the
Communist takeover, work groups in the area were assigned

sections to excavate with shovels and buckets. It was a massive endeavour, accomplished by forced "volunteer" labour during the workers' leisure hours.

My grandfather's house was only a few blocks from this park. The original building had been set back from the road, but as we approached on foot, I saw an ugly one-storey addition, a phone card/photocopy shop, extending out to the sidewalk. My cousin said that if I had come ten years earlier, I would have seen a garden in front of the house, with a path leading up to the front door. He sounded sad but resigned. I stood and looked at the free-standing, two-storey brick dwelling, which had been owned by my grandfather and then inherited by Big Uncle. From the sidewalk I could now see only its top half, but under the gable peak I discerned a faint trace of some characters that had once been affixed to the brick. Kung told me that the characters were Big Uncle's name. During the Cultural Revolution, the Red Guards had knocked the characters off, ridding China of these vestiges of a classed society that believed in property ownership. This was the house where Big Uncle had brought his bride, my mother's *thoh*, and where they had lived for several years before moving into the five-storey mansion that he would build in Canton.

Big Uncle should have left China earlier, said Kung. Perhaps then he might have been able to move some of his assets. But he had kept praying for a Kuomintang victory, and in the end, he left with only a small fraction of his shrinking wealth. Big Uncle had often talked about his belief in investing in real estate, that property was tangible and everlasting. His mistake was that he'd invested only in Canton, had too much faith in the Kuomintang and underestimated the Communists. Everyone in my family had been deeply affected by history: the Second World War, the Communist takeover, the Cultural Revolution. Implicit in all the tales they told me was how fortunate I had been to spend my life insulated from China's political and social upheavals.

We walked around the block to look at the rear of the house, which backed directly onto the road. Across the street, behind my mother's childhood home, were three- and four-storey apartment buildings that appeared modern, yet neglected, with laundry hanging from bamboo poles on every balcony. My cousin explained that when our mothers were children, the area had been filled with leafy bamboo groves and fields of rice and vegetables—idyllic surroundings. Yet the place was dangerous. He asked me if I knew our grandfather had been murdered. As I nodded, he started to tell me his version of the story. Our grandfather had been called into a local bank for a medical emergency, and when he came out, some marauding soldiers mistook his black medical case for a bag stuffed with money. They dragged him into the bamboo grove near his house and bludgeoned him to death. The story was similar to my mother's, although some details were different. According to her, he'd been returning home from a house call and had gone into a teahouse to socialize with friends.

I looked at my grandfather's house again. It was built of solid brick, with plumbing and electricity, which would have been regarded as modern at the time. It was not a large house, but neither was it small. He gave his children a middle-class life in what would then have been a happy setting. But even with his skills, with his respected position as an herbalist doctor, he could not shield them from the inhumanity of life in early-twentieth-century China. I cannot begin to imagine the sickening horror my mother and her family must have felt upon finding their beloved father's crumpled body in that peaceful stand of bamboo, where my mother and Little Aunt would have laughed and played almost every day.

My cousin and I had grown up on the same stories. He suggested that we walk to the church where our mothers had attended Sunday school. It was only a short distance from the house, an easy walk for a young child. The building dated from 1922, but the Chinese Baptist Church had had a presence in the area since 1891. As the lay minister took us through his modest church, I tried to imagine my mother and Little Aunt as children, sitting on low chairs in one of the rooms while the missionaries sang hymns and told stories from the Bible. I could see my mother, small and bright, so eager to learn. She loved to tell me how much the missionaries liked her. She was always the first to master the new stitch in knitting or embroidery. She would then turn and help others like Little Aunt, who were never as smart. Or so she said.

When I used to return home from Sunday school at the Presbyterian church in Acton, I would often absentmindedly sing or hum the hymns from the morning service. My mother sometimes echoed them in Chinese. In my mind I can still hear her singing in that pure, sweet voice, *Yay-su oiy gnoy*, Jesus loves me, this I know . . . .

The marble floors in my cousin's living room felt cool against my feet. Michael and I were sitting on a low, rosewood bench, and Lin had brought out a plate of watermelon. My relatives never stopped eating. Kung pointed to a photograph under a sheet of glass that covered his coffee table and asked if I recognized one of the girls in the picture. I peered closely at the sepia image of four young girls and saw my mother in the group—perhaps fourteen or fifteen years old. I had never seen a picture of her at such an early age. But there she was, a teenaged girl full of life and anticipation, staring back at me. In another year or so, she would be married to that very no-good man. My mother was sitting on the arm of a carved, wooden bench, while Little Aunt was sitting on a cushion beside her. Another girl, who seemed to be about ten or eleven, sat on the other arm. Kung did not know who she was, but I suspected she was Big Uncle's daughter. She bore a marked resemblance to some photographs I'd seen of her as a young adult. We were unable to identify the fourth person, a young woman standing behind the other three. She was definitely the oldest and the most beautiful. Her shoulder-length hair was thick and permed, and there was a slight smile on her face. She exuded confidence and sensuality. I had to think she was the oldest sister, the one my mother referred to as Family Beauty. And yet, even in the company of such striking young women, it was my mother who held my gaze. Again, there was that familiar compelling stare. My mother and Little Aunt were dressed in identical, loose-fitting *cheongsams*, possibly school uniforms, or perhaps dresses made especially for this occasion.

Everyone in the photograph seemed so relaxed, so middle-class. I remembered the close-up of my father on his head tax certificate, the bewildered expression on his face. I thought about the stories of his indigent childhood and pictured a skinny, cringing adolescent with a wooden yoke across his shoulder, carrying heavy pails of water on blistered shoulders while being scolded by an uncaring and ruthless boss. The people in this picture were living a life beyond that boy's wildest dreams. They possessed the quiet confidence that comes with privilege, a look I had associated with other families but never my own.

My cousin brought me another photo. A woman in her late teens or early twenties sat in a chair. She was wearing a simple, flower-printed *cheongsam*. Seated on the arm of the chair was a man dressed in a suit and tie, with his hand resting protectively on her shoulder. They were both leaning slightly forward and toward each other. The intimacy between them was evident and tender. The woman's resemblance to my mother was remarkable, but she was not my mother. The photo was of Little Aunt and her husband, Kung's parents. As I looked at this photograph, I felt envious. I'd never seen a formal picture of my parents together, nothing that announced them as a couple. The only photograph I'd seen of just the two of them was taken outside my father's laundry in Acton. They were standing apart from each other, both wearing heavy winter coats that were several sizes too large. The droop of their mouths, the sag of their shoulders, nothing about them inspired envy. The wind was whipping strands of my mother's hair across her forehead. I never liked that picture.

Once again, Kung told me how indebted his family felt toward my mother. How during the years that they'd lived in the Mainland under the Communist government, they'd depended upon her generosity, how she faithfully sent money year after year. If it had not been for her, he said, they might have starved. I would hear this refrain over and over many times before our trip was finished, and I'd also heard it many times before. As I held the picture of my cousin's parents in my hand, I thought about what their last years must have been like together in their son's home in Macau, surrounded by family, living in the only culture they had ever known.

During our time in Taishan, Kung insisted on paying for everything from taxi rides to an evening at a hot springs resort. On our last morning, when we went to the station to take the bus to Kaiping City, he insisted on paying the fares for everyone. He finally agreed, though, that when he and his family joined us in my ancestral county, they would be our guests.

EIGHTEEN

My nephew Lew, son of First Brother Hing, lived with his family in a complex of medium-rise, concrete apartment buildings. There was no greenery between the buildings, and each grey tower rose directly from the asphalt. On the pavement near the entrance was a huge, dark blue mound of jeans. A little girl was playing on top of the heap while her mother sat on a stool and snipped the loose threads from each pair of pants. I stopped and exchanged greetings with the woman. The little girl couldn't take her eyes off Michael, but when I offered to take her picture, she hid behind the mountain of denim.

Bing, who was married to my niece Jeen—Lew's sister—had met Kung, Lin, Michael and me at the Kaiping bus station and invited us for lunch at Lew's apartment. Lew lived there with his wife, Wei; their adult son; and his elderly mother, the widow of First Brother. After Bing unlocked the heavy-looking steel front door, he led us up five flights of stairs. I did not expect to enter a spacious apartment with marble floors and big windows overlooking a large balcony. Since I'd always thought my relatives in China were poor, I was pleased to see Lew's comfortable furnishings: a wooden sofa, a coffee table and a TV. His standard of living was perhaps not as high as Kung's, but possessions like those were not even part of my early childhood in Acton.

The unmistakable aroma of simmering soup filled the air, and in spite of my full breakfast, I felt hungry. Every morning, Jeen, who had lost her job and now received a small pension, arrived before Lew and Wei left for work, to look after their mother. But today she had also been busy preparing lunch.

I had met First Brother's Widow briefly last year when she'd visited us with her son and daughter-in-law at the Ever Joint Hotel. Her face seemed to be lifted from ancient China with her high cheekbones and plucked hairline. But during the past year, the old woman had grown even more frail and was no longer able to climb the five flights of stairs. She had not left the apartment for almost a year.

Jeen wheeled a large, round table with collapsible legs into the middle of the living room, set it up and spread a tablecloth on top. As soon as Lew and Wei arrived home from work, they greeted us and then changed out of their work clothes and started to cook. They told me that Chinese workers, at least in the Kaiping area, were given a two-hour break for lunch. I was astonished and when I told them that most workers in Canada had only thirty to sixty minutes, they both shook their heads. Two hours, they insisted, were necessary for producing a decent meal.

Jeen rolled her eyes and laughed. "Nobody is as fussy as Lew, except Wei," she said. "Wei insists all her vegetables be cut in a particular way and when she cuts up fruit, everything has to be displayed just so. First the fruit has to be carefully chosen, and presented in a way that looks so good your hand automatically reaches out." Wei had gone into the kitchen, and I could hear her good-natured laugh above the hiss of ingredients being tossed into a wok of hot oil.

I once read that food for the Chinese is like sex for Westerners. My relatives were obsessed with food. Since arriving in Macau, we had consumed three multi-course meals every day and snacked in between.

Once Michael and I sat down at the table, Jeen set a large, steaming bowl of watercress soup in the middle. She'd arrived at her brother's early in the morning to get a head start on simmering the stock of pork bones, dried red dates and dried orange peel. Wei carefully ladled out a bowl for each person. After the soup Lew and Wei started bringing out dish after dish. My nephew had gone to much trouble and expense to provide us with an elaborate lunch. There was roast pork from the barbeque shop, a plate of stir-fried shrimp, a whole steamed fish with scallions, a variety of Chinese greens and a steamed patty of minced pork and salted fish with ginger. Jeen had made this last dish because she'd remembered from last year that it was a favourite of Michael Uncle. We ate everything with bowls of hot steamed rice. After a short break Wei produced a platter of perfectly sliced oranges, dragon fruit and Chinese pears. I was deeply touched.

Once lunch was over Michael hooked up his digital camera to Lew's television and showed everyone the photos we'd taken in Taishan and Macau. My relatives commented politely. *Very nice . . .* But the moment anyone in the room appeared on the TV screen, they started to laugh and point at the screen. It didn't matter that Michael spoke no Chinese. He'd crossed the language barrier. When they saw pictures of our granddaughter, they asked how could she, with her blue eyes and fair hair, possibly be one-quarter Chinese? I had wondered the same thing.

Later in the afternoon my sister Jook and her daughter Kim arrived at the apartment. My sister struck me as being slightly more stooped than when I'd last seen her, but Kim was the same, greeting me with her silvery smile. I told my relatives that I wanted to return to my father's village and to the family store in Cheong Hong See. I looked forward to exploring my ancestral village without being rushed from one destination to another. Last year I'd wanted to walk among the rice paddies behind Ning Kai Lee, but there was not enough time. I wanted to return to my father's house and make an offering to the ancestors again. They told me not to worry, that they would look after everything.

It was the beginning of October, but the temperatures in southern China made it feel like July in southern Ontario. Once settled back into the Ever Joint Hotel, Michael and I decided to walk along the river toward the centre of the city.

Last year we were always shuttled by van from one place to another and I'd formed my impressions of this place through the window of a moving vehicle. I remembered Kaiping as rundown and grimy. This evening, for the first time, I saw the beauty of this city, built at the confluence of two large rivers. We walked along the tree-lined boulevard next to the river, then sat down on a bench under a thick canopy of branches and watched the light on the water change as the sun moved closer and closer to the horizon. Several antiquated-looking sampans were moored along the bank. There was something organic about their appearance; in the dimming light the little boats started to look more and more like sea creatures rising out of the river. The air was beginning to cool, and I smelled dampness in the descending dark.

❧

I should not have been surprised. The next morning, the van that Kim had booked for us stopped in front of the hotel, jammed beyond capacity. It already held eleven people. Everyone was headed for Cheong Hong See, the town that I'd discovered, last year, was my actual place of birth. Afterwards, we would go to Ning Kai Lee. Through the van's windows, I could see Kim and Jeen waving and smiling. Crammed in the back two rows were Kung, Lin, Jook and Lew's wife, Wei. There were also a few people I recognized but could not name. Shaking my head, I glanced at my husband, who merely shrugged his shoulders. A grinning Bing hopped out of the front passenger seat and gestured for

Michael to sit down. Attitudes had not changed in the inter-
vening year. Everyone cheerfully reorganized themselves
while Bing and I squeezed inside. Except for my husband,
no one wore a seatbelt. My relatives remembered this from
last year and once again they joked about Michael Uncle's
concern for safety.

Michael has an uncanny sense of direction. Several years
can pass before he returns to a destination he has driven to
only once, and he always seems to know where to go without
the assistance of a map. The moment we left the hotel, he
knew which road to turn down and recalled landmarks that
I had forgotten. Our driver this time was a heavy-set man
who leaned on the horn incessantly, and like the driver the
year before, insisted on passing everything in sight. But this
driver was equally at home passing vehicles from either left
or right. Once again, I noticed my husband's rigid posture
and his fist wrapped tightly around the door handle.

We were driving through a now-familiar landscape of rice,
vegetables, bananas, sugar cane and papayas. My nieces and
cousin Kung kept telling me stories about how remittance
money from overseas relatives had made the townspeople in
Taishan and Kaiping lazy and indifferent to employment. But
this land outside Kaiping City was intensely cultivated and
carefully maintained, evidence that at least the farmers continued to work hard. I was not surprised when Michael
pointed out the approach to Cheong Hong See. At the
entrance to the town, crouching workers were trimming poles
by hand on the ground in a bamboo-processing yard, and
water buffalo were grazing along the road.

During my childhood I heard certain place names over and over again. Ning Kai Lee was our ancestral village; Cheong Hong See was the location of my parents' store. But my mother would often tell me that our store was in Chek Sui. I found this confusing, but this year, when I arrived in Cheong Hong See, Bing also referred to the store being in Chek Sui. He then explained to me that Cheong Hong See was simply a local name, given to our side of the river.

My father's building was in somewhat better shape this year. The outside walls had recently been whitewashed and seemed less tired. But the inside was unchanged: the shelves were still a jumble of dusty boxes packed with old hardware, the tin ceiling shedding flakes of paint. I wondered if the store had sold anything since my previous visit. The proprietor and his wife sat in the very same spot behind the counter. I swore they hadn't moved in a year.

Bing asked if I wanted to see the upstairs. I nodded, pleased that he'd anticipated my unspoken wish. The year before, when I'd inquired about seeing the second floor, someone had muttered that it was unsafe. And I remembered my sister's bemused expression when I had asked to see a place that had been uninhabited for so long. It was the room where I'd been born, but it was worthless as far as she was concerned.

Bing led us back outside and unlocked a door beside the entrance to the store. I braced myself for a space that would be small, confined and dark, yet another reminder of the meagre lives my parents had led. We followed Bing up a narrow set of stairs, which took a turn and opened into a wide staircase with elegant, hand-carved, wooden banisters and spindles. The room was large, with high, peaked ceilings and windows at both ends. It was airy and full of light—not at all what I had imagined. This shabby space had at one time been beautiful. I stood staring, almost breathless, stunned by what I saw. I wandered into each of the three bedrooms, some still containing old dusty furniture. Jeen pointed to an armoire and said it had been built for her parents' wedding. At one time this cast-off cupboard had been exquisite, with colourful images of flowers and fruit painted on black lacquer.

In one of the bedrooms, Michael noticed a Western-style wardrobe trunk, reinforced in the corners with brass fittings, a trunk similar to the ones his parents had used when they'd crossed the Atlantic from England. I smiled when Jook called it a Gold Mountain chest; it had belonged to our father and had crossed the Pacific many times. On his return journey to China in the late 1920s, he'd made a stopover in Hong Kong, where he filled the trunk with books of classical Chinese literature. After the death of First Wife, just after the start of the Second World War, First Brother sold all the books and used the money to satisfy his gambling addiction. I felt a rush of anger when I heard this story, but my sister spoke without rancour.

Above the travel trunk was a wooden picture frame crowded with photos. Kim was standing beside me and pointed at one corner. "That's you when you were just a girl. And look at this one of you and Michael Uncle with your daughters when they were babies. First Brother Uncle must have put these pictures together. He and his family lived here after your mother left for Hong Kong with you, your sister and Doon Uncle." I had not expected this, not pictures of me with my husband and children. My mother had sent pictures here too, and even though the recipients had not met many of the people in the photos, they were put on display for others to see, for others to know that this family was blessed with a Gold Mountain benefactor.

As I looked around, I became keenly aware that this apartment had belonged to a well-off man. It stood in such stark contrast to the dark, cramped house in Ning Kai Lee. My father had intended that he and my mother would spend the rest of their lives in this spacious, comfortable home. Nothing in these surroundings matched what I knew about my parents. Was it possible that once my father returned to China and married my mother, they'd decided to build a life together here, perhaps without romance, but at least with maturity and mutual respect?

But then the Communists arrived, and my mother knew that the life she was enjoying with her young daughters and stepsons in the market town of Cheong Hong See was about to end. Everyone told her how lucky she was to have a husband in Gam Sun, someone who gave her the means to leave the country legally. People were fearful of the Communists, and my mother suspected that life under their regime would be harsh. Sooner or later they would have found out about her connection to Big Uncle and our very survival would have been at risk.

Her preference would have been for only his sons to join him in Canada. She and her daughters would live in Hong Kong and receive remittances from my father. But the better schools were beyond his means, and Canada offered free education. The time had come to join him overseas.

My brother, Shing, once told me that our father did not want to return to Canada where he would have to *su lo fon hai*. I knew exactly what he meant, but it was one of those phrases for which I had no precise translation. The closest I could offer Michael was that our father dreaded a future where every breath he took was filled with the contempt of *lo fons*. He no longer wanted to fill his lungs with that bitter, toxic air. In 1947, when he believed he was returning to China to stay, his feelings of joy and hope must have been euphoric. The war was over and he would finally be reunited with his children. He would marry a woman whom he respected. Together, they would put the anguish of those war years behind and build a new life in Cheong Hong See. A few short years later he made his no-choice journey back to the Gold Mountain, a man weighed down by anger and despair.

While I stood in my parents' apartment in Cheong Hong See, Jook told me that in our village our father was *mung kah lah*. When I heard this I could have wept. *Mung kah lah* was how my mother described Big Uncle. Powerful. The image I

have of my father is of a small man with his head perpetu-
ally bent at a slight angle while he worked: sorting dirty
laundry, ironing rumpled laundry, pulling wet laundry out of
the washing machine. It was labour performed always with
one's head down, always looking at one's hands. As I looked
back I understood what I could not articulate as a child. My
father was a man who carried the look of defeat. I saw it in
his wilted mouth, the slump of his shoulders, in the way his
feet barely left the ground when he walked. If my parents
agreed on anything, it was that fate had never smiled upon
them. In retrospect that brief window of happiness in Cheong
Hong See seems almost cruel. Given that my father persisted
all those years with eking out a living in sad hand laundries,
driven by his all-consuming sense of duty, his efforts were
nothing short of heroic.

My father managed to find one *lo fon* friend in the town of
Allandale. I think for men like my father it wasn't just the
overt racism that weighed on their spirits; it was knowing
that as far as the larger community was concerned, they
didn't exist. My father knew that as long as he did lowly,
unthreatening work like washing clothes, the *lo fons*, by and
large, would leave him alone. But not always. He sometimes
talked about his early years in Canada when he had to dodge
those *sei gwei doys*, those half-dead ghost boys, who were
after his money. He used to pick up dirty laundry in a cloth
sack, and after it had been washed, pressed and folded, he
returned it wrapped in brown paper. On delivery days, he
was always looking over his shoulder, watchful of the ghost

boys who might overtake him and rob him of the little money he had collected.

My father met Mr. Ward, the only name I've ever known him by, when he took a clock in for repair at Mr. Ward's jewellery and watch repair shop. Later, when Mr. Ward brought the mended clock to the laundry, my father, struggling to make himself understood, pointed to the square outline on the dusty shelf where the clock had stood and shook his head. Mr. Ward looked at the round base and understood that he had delivered the wrong clock. Years later, when I heard the account from Mr. Ward's son, he told it with a smile on his face. As a child I was baffled as to why the adults found this story funny.

When my father started to sponsor family members to Canada, he asked for Mr. Ward's help with negotiating the maze of immigration bureaucracy. Mr. Ward had died before I arrived in Allandale, but my father spoke fondly of this man who had taken the time to help him fill out forms and to buy money orders to send to China. When his friend died, my father bought a wreath for his funeral—a gesture of profound respect and generosity from a man who deprived himself of even the smallest luxury.

The friendship with the Ward family continued after Mr. Ward's death, and a few days after my mother and I arrived in Allandale, Mr. Ward's son and his wife visited the laundry. They took me to Sunday school and enrolled me at the local public school, and on Saturdays I watched television with their daughter, who was several years older than I was. Just before we moved to Acton, they came to the laundry to say goodbye; Mrs. Ward was crying. She gave my father a letter to give to the teacher at my new school. Each summer they made the long drive to fetch me and take me to their cottage near Kempenfelt Bay. During those weeks, I played in the water, hiked in the woods and memorized the English names of wildflowers, birds and trees. Mr. and Mrs. Ward laughed a lot; they never fought.

NINETEEN

My mother often spoke fondly about a family friend she called *Brother* Mau. Earlier in the day, Jeen had told me that *Brother* Mau and First Brother Hing had been students in my mother's school. I'd had no idea of that. Not only did my father hire my mother, but she had taught his oldest son. This was a part of family lore, Jeen told me. She shook her head in amazement at my ignorance.

Brother Mau had not been smart in school, but my mother had liked him because of his sweet temper and his willingness to help others and work. He had died several years before I returned to China. After we left my parents' apartment in Chong Hong See we drove to Ning Kai Lee. Mau's two sons and his grandsons were waiting for us on the paved forecourt at the village entrance. They led us down a narrow path between the grey brick houses toward my father's house. Although we were not accompanied by a large contingent from the village this year, everyone we met knew who we were and why we had come.

I stopped every so often to glance at the rooftops. The ornamental dragons were still there, jutting out into graceful curves beyond the peaks of the roofs, guarding the inhabitants against evil spirits, so different from Kung's village. Again I felt thankful that poverty had at least shielded these buildings from the fervour of the Red Guards.

The squatter still lived in the front room of my father's house. Clothes were still hanging on a rod, suspended from the ceiling. The same bicycle was propped against a wall. But the room felt more cluttered. Perhaps there was an extra chair or two. The middle room remained unused. My nieces were arranging bowls of fruit, cooked meat and cups of tea on a table in front of the altar. I was still shocked by the primitive surroundings. Once more, I felt a sadness in the air, and now that I'd seen the large apartment above the store in Cheong Hong See, it was almost crushing. The hole in the roof had been patched, at least, and I asked Michael to take a picture so my brothers could see the repair.

Jeen struck a match and lit the sticks of incense. She turned to Michael and me and gave each of us a bundle. I bowed three times before the shrine, hoping the ancestors had remembered our offering from the year before. Once we finished, I gave each village relative a red envelope with fifty yuan for good luck. I had wanted to give them each a hundred, but Jeen and Kim had protested and said that was too much. We then left to walk around the village.

Brother Mau's oldest son was keen to show us his home. It was one of the few modern ones in Ning Kai Lee. With three floors, electricity and running water, it was a modest version of the house my cousin Kung had built outside Taishan. Oldest Son had been born after my mother left the village, yet he knew all about my parents. Once again, I heard the stories about the schoolteacher with the elevated background who'd married the learned Gold Mountain guest. Oldest Son took us to his balcony. We emerged to see all the neighbouring rooftops beneath us; they were so close I felt as if I could hop from one clay-tiled roof to another. All around us in the hazy distance were more, similarly compact villages, surrounded by the same green fields and low hills. After chatting with us for a while, Oldest Son reminded Kim that his mother wanted to meet us.

Kim led me through the narrow alleys back to the centre of the village. Michael and my other relatives headed out into the adjacent rice fields. Kim and I arrived to find a woman in her eighties sitting on a low, wooden stool next to her door. Though her house was smaller, Widow Mau's grey brick home was not unlike the one that belonged to my family. Outside the entrance to her home lay a pile of sticks, fuel for the brick cooking hearth in her kitchen.

Widow Mau was a stout woman; her grey hair, still abundant, was parted at the side and combed behind her ears. Her hands looked large, and the soles of her bare feet were rough and calloused. And like my sister and every Chinese woman of a similar vintage, she was dressed in pyjama-style pants and a loose blouse. She knew who I was and immediately greeted me with the familiar refrain about that mythical couple: my clever mother who was the best schoolteacher the village had ever had and my respected father, a man of great learning and much generosity. She told me that *Brother* Mau and First Brother had been students together in my mother's class, then added with a chuckle that Mau had not been good at school but my mother had been fond of him nonetheless. I listened and nodded politely, even though Jeen had just told me all of this.

After the birth of each of his children, Mau had written to my mother in Canada and asked her to bestow a name. And while my parents were alive, they sent money at every Chinese New Year. The widow said that my father was a good man. He'd sent money to many of the poorest families in the village. She then shook her head in disgust and started talking about my father's brother, Second Uncle, who had gone to Canada with my father in 1914. "Did you know that Second Uncle came home from the Gold Mountain only once?" I shook my head and she continued. "Fathered a daughter here and then never came back. And he never sent money home. Did you know that it was your father who sent money to Second Uncle's wife and daughter? Now Second Uncle had bought farmland, and with the harvest, his wife and daughter were able to live, but your father's money made life easier for them." Her voice dropped to a whisper. "People say that in the Gold Mountain, he had taken a *gwei poh*, a ghost woman, that he spent all his money on her. He wasn't like your father, the best man to come out of this village. There was no one better than your father." Mau's widow wagged her finger at me to emphasize this last point.

"Yes, yes, it's true," said Kim, nodding her head.

My mouth had gone dry with listening to this story. All my life the man I'd heard referred to as Second Uncle had been a mystery. By the time my mother and I arrived in Canada in 1955, my father's older brother had been dead for almost ten years, and apart from his place of birth, I knew almost nothing about him. My mother sometimes whispered to me that my father's brother had gone crazy and ended up in an insane asylum. The few times that my father did speak to me about his older brother, the words always caught in his throat and his face took on a look of unbearable sadness. While Mau's widow spoke, I kept thinking of my father. With gut-wrenching loyalty, he had kept all these unflattering things about his brother to himself.

I had always imagined Second Uncle as a tragic figure, going mad far from home in a cold, lonely land, where every day offered nothing but drudgery. Even after hearing what Mau's widow had to say about him, I still found Second Uncle's story moving. Whether the rumour about him and a *gwei poh* is true or not I will never know. And if it is true, I pray that he at least found comfort in that intimacy, however brief it might have been. I was almost glad to hear about his "selfish" behaviour. To me, my father was *too* generous, *too* selfless, *too* duty-bound. He left nothing for himself.

Mau's widow could tell that I was intrigued and seemed quite pleased that she could tell me something I did not know. She continued: *Brother* Mau's father was my father's oldest brother, and he remained in China while my father and Second Uncle went to the Gold Mountain. This made *Brother* Mau and me cousins. *Why had my parents never told me about this older brother, who would have been First Uncle?* I knew that my father had other siblings, sisters who had married out of the village, but I had never heard about a brother other than Second Uncle. I noticed that Kim was silent, smiling with her lips clamped together, almost grimacing. Something was not right.

A few days later she would tell me that she'd checked out the Widow Mau's story with her mother. Jook had replied that *Brother* Mau's father was not a blood brother to my father. He'd been adopted, to replace the oldest brother, who had died, and thus Mau's children were not true relatives. Kim was upset that Mau's widow had lied and that I'd given her money as a relative. But I didn't care. These people had so little. To them I must have seemed like a millionaire. I couldn't blame Mau's widow, for the sake of her own family, for wanting to establish closer kinship with me, a modern-day Gold Mountain guest.

The sun was still high in the sky. The temperatures were comfortable, without the humidity of the previous year. After Kim and I left Widow Mau, I found Michael and the others on the paths between the rice fields surrounding the village. My husband was bent over, examining some leaves. Bing and Kung were standing next to him, gesturing, obviously trying to explain something about the plant. Michael suddenly grinned, and I knew that they'd managed to communicate.

By North American standards, the fields were small, but they were intensely cultivated. Kim told me the growing season continued year-round. With the others following, Jook caught up to us and took my hand. Together we walked from one field to another, as I had wanted to do last year. I turned and looked back at my father's little village. Yes, this community was impoverished, but under the intense blue sky, the simple grey-brick houses and the surrounding sea of lush, green rice paddies seemed like a picture composed for a postcard. There were no modern buildings, no electricity poles or wires in sight. It could not have been much different when my father was a boy. In the distance, low hills were catching the late afternoon sun. My niece Jeen pointed to them. "Over there, that's where your grandparents are buried and your First Mother."

My First Mother? What was Jeen talking about? I was about to say something, and then . . . Of course. In Chinese culture, if you belonged to the same family, you would always have a title that would explain your relationship. The woman buried in those hills was my father's first wife, and therefore *my* first mother. It made no difference *who* my biological mother was. First Wife would always be number one.

I wanted to rush over, to climb that hill and visit First Mother's grave, but Jeen put a hand on my shoulder and said it was not advisable. Grave-visiting ceremonies traditionally took place in the spring, and such an event had to be carefully planned. Jeen needed to look at the calendar, find an auspicious date and make plans for a proper offering. Jook nodded in agreement. I would have to wait.

TWENTY

K ung and Lin had returned to Macau the previous evening, and Jeen was staying behind at Lew's apartment to look after her mother. The others had to work. So Kim and Bing were appointed by the family to escort us around Chikan, the closest town of any significance to Cheong Hong See. I soon discovered the streets were lined with impressive but neglected historic architecture, three- and four-storey buildings, ornately decorated with plaster friezes, pillars and curved balconies, evidence of the town's heyday in the twenties and thirties. Like so many in the Four Counties, it had once become prosperous because of overseas money.

The town was constructed along both banks of a river that eventually flowed through Kaiping City before joining the Pearl and flowing into the South China Sea. The waterway was dotted with sampans, barely holding together and definitely not seaworthy. Yet the dogs tied up on their decks, the jumbles of furniture and hanging laundry all signalled that these were undeniably permanent dwellings. Bing explained that many of the town's residents belonged to two rival families, the Gunns and the Setos. He pointed to an imposing clock tower built by the Setos and a more recent one constructed by the Gunns that was even bigger and more elaborate. Bing found this rivalry amusing and later told me that he was a member of the Seto clan.

We spent the afternoon trailing after Bing as he led us through narrow side streets, pointing out buildings that had been abandoned just before the arrival of the Communists, rich people's homes that he had later explored as a child. Sometimes he wandered into rooms still fully furnished; at the time people were hoping the Communist regime would be a temporary setback and that they would return fairly soon to their old properties and resume their lives. Toward the end of the afternoon, we walked to the town library, which had been built by the Setos. With his affable manner, Bing introduced himself to the library keeper and arranged for us to have a tour of the building. During the war, when the Japanese had occupied the town, they chose the library as their headquarters.

According to my mother, the people in my father's village were fortunate because they never fell victim to the Japanese. When the Japanese came to Ning Kai Lee, she said, the villagers escaped to the nearby hills. This, of course, gave her an opening to tell me her hard-luck stories about the adversity she had suffered during the war and throughout her life in general. When I mentioned my mother's comment to Kim, she replied that the Japanese never went past Cheong Hong

See, that they never made it to my father's village. Looking at the splendid buildings in Chikan, I said that Ning Kai Lee had likely been saved because the Japanese could not be bothered with such a tiny, obscure place. Again Kim shook her head at this aunt who seemed so misinformed. "The Japanese never got to our village because they couldn't get past Cheong Hong See," she said. "They were afraid."

The people in my family were born storytellers. It seemed that each one knew how to dangle something before me, and when I expressed disbelief, as the look on my face right then certainly did, the answer would always be the same: you don't understand; you don't know. Kim continued, her tone telling me to stay quiet and listen. "During the war there was a statue of the goddess Kuan-Yin standing outside a temple at the entrance to Cheong Hong See. The Japanese were about to march through the town, but the horses leading the column of troops refused to pass the temple. They reared up on their hind legs, whinnying and neighing, then finally knelt before the altar and would not budge, not even when the riders got off and whipped them. The officers of the brigade were so spooked that they turned back to Chikan. So they never went on to Ning Kai Lee."

"Is the temple still there?" I inquired, wanting to see it.

"No. No. The Communists destroyed the temple and the statue a long time ago." Kim said this with a wave of the hand, dismissing my unspoken request for evidence.

Kim had not been born when this had supposedly happened and had heard the account only from others, but as far as she was concerned, that made no difference to the veracity of the story. "It's true. Everyone says so," she said with a rising voice as if each telling made the story more credible. Her explanation was riveting, but it also had the unmistakable whiff of a tall tale. The skeptic in me suspected that if the Japanese had wanted to expand their occupation, their efforts would not have been thwarted by a statue of Kuan-Yin. To me, this was as likely as the story that my mother had chased my father. But my niece, even though these events occurred years before her birth, spoke with the conviction of a true believer.

Lew was born after my mother, Doon, Ming Nee and I had left Mainland China, while we were living in Hong Kong. My mother never met him, and yet of all her step-grandchildren in China, she seemed to love him the most. She would mention his name more than any other, and he was specifically left a small inheritance in her will. I never thought much about their relationship. It was one of those mysterious things connected to China and had nothing to do with me.

I was getting used to the five flights of stairs leading to Lew's apartment. Bing had come to the Ever Joint Hotel earlier that morning to invite us for lunch. We'd happily accepted. When Michael and I entered the apartment, First Brother's Widow was seated by the window in her usual place. I sat down beside her and held her hand in mine. Within a few moments Lew and Wei arrived home from work. As expected they changed and started to cook. Jeen had already put on a pot of soup. The distinct aroma of medicinal herbs simmering in the chicken stock reminded me of my childhood. Several times a week my mother used to fill a pot with water and pork or chicken bones and a variety of dried herbs, roots and seeds meant to fortify blood, improve circulation or clear the lungs.

Delicious smells filled the room. Jeen had taken a tray of food to her mother, and everyone else was seated at the round table. Once again, Jeen brought out a steamed patty made from minced salted fish, pork and ginger, which she presented to my husband. "Michael Uncle likes this. I remember," she said, then waited for me to translate.

Michael grinned, picked up his chopsticks, broke off a piece and popped it into his mouth. "*Ho sec*, delicious," he said. Everyone around the table cheered.

Partway through our meal, Jeen inquired whether I knew about a brother who "lives above my head." *A brother who lives above my head?* But in that very instant, I understood that Jeen was referring to a son my mother had given birth to the year before I was born. He had lived only a few days. I had always known about this child but rarely thought about him.

After I nodded in answer to her question, Jeen asked, "Did you know that if it hadn't been for Lew, your mother would never have made it to Canada?" Once again, I felt as if a carrot was being dangled in front of me. Without waiting for a reply, Jeen went on. "When your mother was in Hong Kong with Ming Nee and you, the Canadian government had twice refused her application to enter Canada."

"*Jin hai-lah?*" I said—*Really?*—not so much as a response, but as a signal for her to continue.

"Well, your mother decided to see a fortune teller. The fortune teller said that it was the spirit of her dead son who was preventing her from leaving the country. He was upset with his mother for leaving China and with the prospect that there was no one to carry on his lineage. Well, our mother, First Brother's wife, was pregnant at the time. Your mother was told to adopt this child as her dead son's offspring and make him her grandchild. So after Lew was born, we had a ceremony, making him the spirit son of your dead brother. This made the brother "who lives above your head" happy and shortly afterward the Canadian government granted your mother permission to enter. You can say whatever you want, but as soon as your dead brother got his son, your mother got the necessary papers." I glanced over at First Brother's Widow, and she nodded.

I might have guessed that my mother would seek the advice of a clairvoyant. She was never a religious person, and yet I would be hard pressed to find someone more superstitious. She paid close attention to a person's moles, convinced that an unlucky position could spell misfortune. She believed in *hai thleng*, which translates roughly as face reading. But *hai thleng* was more than that. It was the belief that by examining facial contours, the shape and symmetry of features, by reading a person's *chi*, a fortune teller could not only see goodness or evil, but could also foresee the course of a person's life.

My father often used to tell me that in Chinese society, one always felt stronger kinship toward the father's side of the family. This was why parents were always cared for by sons and not daughters. My mother retorted that we were living in the West and that none of those customs applied— though she did not dismiss those beliefs herself. Little by little my mother's behaviour was beginning to make sense: the letters and the money that she sent to Lew, her insistence that this man whom she had never met be included in her will. I now understood why Lew treated me with such respect, why we had been invited so many times to his home for meals, why he and Wei made special trips to deliver late evening soup to us at our hotel. I looked across the table at my *spirit* nephew. For a moment our eyes met.

TWENTY-ONE

Michael unfolded the Chinese-language Kaiping tourist map and laid it on the desk in our hotel room. Earlier in the day, Bing had pointed out all the sites we had visited, and my husband then carefully circled the names and wrote down the English transliterations.

Bing had told us that the northern part of Kaiping County was quite different from the south. Fewer people from there had travelled overseas, and the people from the south generally considered it to be a backwater. He knew all this because he'd been sent there for re-education during the Cultural Revolution.

Michael pored over the map and noticed that the elevations in the northern section of the county were higher and that there were fewer roads. It indeed appeared to be an area of little development. I decided that I wanted to see it. I had returned to China to learn more about my parents, to get to know my family better. But there was more . . . Although I knew I was likely seeking something intangible that perhaps

237

no longer existed, I was looking for the China that had belonged to my parents. If, in fact, it were to be found, it would be in small, unexpected glimpses. I convinced myself that if I gathered together enough of these vignettes, I might be able to patch together a quilt of mental images. And that would give me a suggestion of the China they had once called home.

Kim and Bing hired yet another van to take us to Ai Sah, the most northern town in the county. From there we would explore the countryside and hike into the mountains. When the van arrived at the hotel, Kim's younger sister, Su, and her husband, Ven, were with them as well. I had become used to new people materializing just for these excursions.

Ven was a senior civil servant with a well-paying job that would eventually give him a government pension. He seemed to be the relative with the most status, a man whom everyone respected. I had observed during family gatherings that whenever he spoke, people listened. When he heard about our trip, he decided to take the day off work and accompany us. He had also asked a friend in the area to reserve a table at a local restaurant that specialized in wild game.

Su is a gentle woman in her mid-forties. Being ten years younger than her sister, she was not as severely affected by the political turmoil of the Cultural Revolution. She was able to complete her education and went on to train as an herbal pharmacist. There is a quiet confidence about Su, the manner of someone who is secure in her position. For twenty years she worked for the government, but once laws governing the ownership of property were relaxed, she bought a shop in the market town of Ong Sun, a few miles south of Cheong Hong

See. Her store, which Michael, my brothers and I had visited the year before, is a large, quiet space with a feeling of calm and order. Two of the walls are lined with wooden drawers, filled with dried roots, leaves, seeds, berries, dried geckos, seahorses and ground deer antlers. An L-shaped glass counter holds even more packages of Chinese herbal medicines. During our visit I'd watched her serve customers, listening to their symptoms, opening drawers, carefully scooping out ingredients to be weighed on a hand-held scale and finally wrapping everything in crisp, white paper tied together with thin, red string. I often wondered if Su's life was what my mother had at one time possessed, working behind the counter of the store in Cheong Hong See. Oddly enough, my niece with her overbite and intelligent eyes actually looks like my mother, yet they are not related by blood.

As we travelled north out of Kaiping City, the land started to rise and the sandy soil turned a rich, ochre colour. Over time the hillsides had been dramatically sculpted into large, terraced rice paddies. From a distance they looked like giant steps, carpeted with crops of ripening rice, the green stalks gently swaying in a humid haze. As the city fell farther and farther behind us, the villages became more dilapidated. Most of the houses were constructed from yellow mud bricks, rather than the familiar narrow grey ones. I'd also become accustomed to seeing rural dwellings built on a grid, with the walls of the outside homes forming the perimeter of a village compound. But many of these houses seemed randomly situated, with meandering paths between them. The hamlets were nestled against verdant hills and cold mountain streams, and they looked magical despite the obvious poverty.

I noticed a winding dirt path between some of the terraced fields, and asked the driver to stop so that Michael and I could explore. As we were walking, Michael noticed a Paris Peacock, a velvet black butterfly with flashes of iridescent blue and red in each wing, almost the size of a hummingbird. As soon as he saw this butterfly he tried to photograph it, but found it extremely difficult because of its tendency to hover rather than settle while feeding. We then heard Bing rushing to catch up with us. Since there was no signpost, we were not aware that there was a village at the end of the road. Just as Bing arrived, a man appeared, apparently out of nowhere, and confronted us. Bing quickly spoke up and said that we had travelled from overseas to study Chinese butterflies and pointed at Michael's field guide and camera. The man hesitated for a moment, then left.

Bing later told us that some of the people in these remote communities had likely never even been to Kaiping City, much less seen a *lo fon*. We were only about ninety minutes from the county capital, and yet some of these people may have spent a lifetime venturing no more than a few miles from their birthplace. In cities like Shenzhen, the development couldn't move fast enough; here, time seemed to have stood still.

The outdoor market at Ai Sah was raucous with the sounds of dogs barking, fowls squawking and people calling attention to their offerings. We walked up and down aisles where mats were laid on the ground, crowded with items for sale: chickens, ducks, geese, frogs tied by their legs into groups of three and four, dogs in cages, vegetables, fruit, various dried foods, seeds, clothing, snakes, hats, pots and pans. The owners who crouched next to their wares and produce stared as our group walked past and beckoned to us, hoping we would stop. Except for the plastic tarpaulins covering the ground instead of woven bamboo mats and apart from the occasional sound of motorized vehicles, I was sure my parents would have wandered about a market just like this, bargaining for food and other necessities.

Kim passed several chicken merchants before deciding which one to patronize. She squatted without effort and started to scrutinize several of the vendor's birds, clutching them by the feet and touching their bellies and under their wings. She made a point of poking the birds' crops, feeling for evidence that they'd been fed grain. Grain-fed chickens, she told me later, tasted the best. After several minutes she told the seller that her chickens were not very plump. The seller protested indignantly. They argued quietly back and forth for a while, but in the end my niece bought the three that she thought were the best, the fattest.

Even though I believe in using fresh ingredients and rarely buy prepared groceries, compared to my Chinese nieces' and nephews' diets, my food is far removed from its source. Only in the summer can I eat directly from our garden. Kim was

pleased with her purchase and proudly told me that she preferred live fowl. The reason was simple. They tasted better.
Bing and Su each carried a chicken, grabbing it by its wings
and folding them behind its back. The fowl were calm and
quiet, no squawking, no resisting. Bing and Su held the birds
as casually as if they were grocery bags. The previous day
Michael and I had walked through a large, Western-style food
store in Kaiping City, but I could not imagine any of my relatives pushing a metal grocery cart and buying food wrapped
in plastic on a Styrofoam tray.

Ven took the third chicken to the restaurant, where it
would be killed and plucked for our lunch. He would tell the
restaurant owner how he wanted the chicken cooked and
choose the other dishes that would accompany our meal.
These discussions were typical of our outings with the family.
Whenever we went into a restaurant, the host would sit down
with us and tell us what food was available. One of my relatives, usually Kim, would then decide what we wanted, how
it should be cooked and negotiate how much we should pay.
Except in the hotel restaurant, I never looked at a menu.

Michael found a stall where a man was selling hand-
forged, metal billhooks. As he approached, the vendor's eyes
widened, and he held out one of his utensils for inspection.
My husband examined a few of them, turning them over
and checking the blades to see that they had a uniform thick-
ness. He then compared the way each knife was curved into
a hook a the tip of the blade. He held several in his hand,
comparing the grip of the handles. My husband turned to
me and said that these knives were exactly what he had been

looking for, just the ticket for cutting those thistles behind our barn. The vendor smiled and made encouraging gestures. Once Michael decided which one he wanted, I asked the merchant for the price. While he told me, he wrote a number on a scrap of paper for Michael's benefit. My husband was about to pay the written amount when Bing, still holding the chicken in his hand, rushed over and scolded the man, telling him that he was charging too much and that it was wrong of him to take advantage simply because the customer was a *lo fon*. He later told us that if we hadn't been there, he would have been able to buy it for even less money. After a moment's polite hesitation, he added that we should never pay the opening price.

"Even for you, it would be high," Bing said to me. "But for Michael Uncle . . . ridiculous!" Bing shook his head, unable to believe that Michael was willing to pay the first suggested amount. It seemed that wherever we went with my relatives, they hovered over us, saving us from an unscrupulous world, eager to take advantage of two defenceless people. As it was, Michael paid the equivalent of 1.44 American dollars. The initial price had been close to two.

Once we returned to the van, Bing took out a pocket knife and cut several holes into a cardboard box before putting the two remaining chickens inside. After the precious cargo was locked in the vehicle, we walked to the restaurant where Ven was waiting.

A table had been set for us on the third floor. Ven had consulted with the owner ahead of time to make sure we'd sample locally caught game. We started with land frog (toad) soup. Later came two dishes wrapped and steamed in lotus leaves. Ven folded the leaves back from one dish and revealed small chunks of frog meat. Kim unwrapped the other package, and inside were chunks of the chicken she had chosen, steamed in a ginger and black bean sauce and arranged in a pattern of concentric circles. There was wild mountain pig stew, fresh fish from a nearby reservoir, local tofu and a variety of vegetable dishes from the restaurant garden. This was not cuisine that I would have chosen to eat. But I knew it had been selected with care, and I knew it would be found nowhere on the tourist map. The aroma was heady and strong. Michael smiled at me, picked up his chopsticks without hesitation and started to eat.

Not long ago Kim had gone to visit a friend who lived in the area and who took her to a place in the mountains called Yellow Olive. She told our driver where she thought it might be, and he knew it was not that far from Ai Sah. We returned to the van and this time drove into the mountains, where the roads became steeper and rougher. We encountered several small villages that again had no signposts indicating their names. The road eventually became so difficult that we told the driver to park while we continued our explorations on foot, taking a well-trodden yellow path that snaked around the mountainside.

At this point I didn't imagine we'd encounter any more villages, but we eventually came across a cluster of dwellings.

A small stream of sparkling water ran beside it, and two people from the village were squatting on the bank, cleaning a chicken. We were surrounded by green terraces filled with rice fields, vegetable gardens and banana groves, all set against a backdrop of misty hills and low mountains. Kim finally recognized a path leading off the main one and led us to another mountain creek that meandered between massive granite boulders, and in some spots left pools of water perfect for swimming. My niece suddenly dipped her head into the water. She encouraged me to do the same, telling me that the mountain water contained minerals that were beneficial for hair. When I declined, she smiled her silvery smile and shrugged her shoulders.

We spent the rest of the afternoon sitting in the sun. Kim pointed out the physical formation that surrounded us: narrow at the top and bottom, wide in the middle. "Just like an olive," she said, "and yellow because of the soil."

I looked around and felt blessed to be able to see this little corner of the world. Colourful butterflies basked in water left in the shallow hollows of the rocks. Bing lit a cigarette and leaned back on a warm rock.

We had left Yellow Olive and were on our way back to the van. Michael was still taking pictures of butterflies, and Bing and Ven had gone on ahead. Su noticed some red berries and peeled one, telling me that it was effective in treating diabetes. I took the offered berry from my niece and bit into it.

The juices tasted tart and made my mouth pucker. My nieces, especially Su, had a great deal of knowledge about the curative qualities of wild plants and herbs and pointed out various medicinal ones growing along the mountain slope. Further along, Kim saw a particular grass and said that it was often boiled to make a brew and then used to bathe jaundiced babies.

When we came to a turn in the path, we stopped for one last chance to gaze at the beauty of Yellow Olive. For a while no one spoke. Then Su said, "Your mother chased my grandfather."

Here we go, I thought to myself. Another village myth about my father, the Gold Mountain guest, and my mother, the schoolteacher with the elevated background. "That's what your mother told me," I finally said.

Kim then added, "Everyone knows our grandfather liked your mother because she was clever. At least that's what *our* mother says. Your mother had knit hats for her and her older brother, Shing Uncle. Doon Uncle was not yet born. People say that our grandfather used to invite your mother to his house for meals. She lived in a dormitory for single women. It wasn't far from my grandfather's house. So she could have a meal with them and go back to her room very easily. People say that my grandmother didn't like your mother."

I glanced at Su, then at Kim. I didn't know what to say. This was new information. I had always thought that until they were married, my parents had had only a professional relationship. It was difficult to picture them being social and friendly with each other. I hesitated, then said, "Well . . . I guess it would be hard to like a woman whom your husband had eyes for." The sisters exchanged a glance. I then added that I didn't blame First Wife.

Su put her hand up to her mouth and giggled. "Many people say that your father wanted to marry your mother soon after they met. Did you know that?" she asked. I immediately stopped looking at the scenery.

Kim rushed in. "I think your father must have liked your mother from the beginning. You see, there was no one else in the village like her. My grandmother, First Wife, was very jealous. My grandfather loved books and learning, and even though your mother was not as beautiful as First Wife, she was educated, someone he could talk to about history and Confucius. He was the one who hired her to teach in the village school. He met with her all the time after the students left. And don't forget First Brother was in her class. He went to discuss business, but the meetings got longer and longer."

My niece paused, as if to gauge my reaction. "Then he started inviting her to his house for dinner—something that First Wife didn't like, but she put up with it. Then . . ." Kim took a breath. "Your father went to a fortune teller and the fortune teller told him he was destined to have two wives. Not only that, but the fortune teller said that the life of First Wife actually depended on his taking a second, that without a second wife in the house, she would die! When my grandfather heard this, he must have thought that First Wife would naturally go along. The gods had spoken. Who would dare go against them?" I had to stop myself from asking Kim to slow down; I didn't want to break the spell. My mind was racing. Was Kim in fact talking about *my parents?*

"Well, my grandfather didn't know First Wife as well as he thought he did. After he told her what the fortune teller prophesized, she grew very angry. She said she saw through him, that it was just an excuse to take that girl from the city as a second wife. Well, she didn't care what the fortune teller said. She didn't believe in that sort of thing. And what if he was just making everything up? She wasn't falling for it. She wanted to be the *only wife*. She would never allow that woman to cross the threshold and become a part of her family. My mother said that people in the village gossiped about it for many years after. Well, you know what happened. My grand-father let First Wife have her way, and she died not long after he returned to Canada."

"That was so terrible," I replied, "those children left on their own." I didn't know what else to say. I wanted to pinch myself. We were back at the van. The driver was leaning against the hood having a cigarette.

These events sounded like something out of a movie. And the notion that my parents actually enjoyed talking to each other seemed inconceivable. I remembered times of compatible conversation, but they were rare. Communication in our home seemed to take the form of either silence or quarrelling. At best, their marriage was a stalemate. And what an unhappy situation for First Wife. Even though she was tall and beautiful, she was no rival for my mother, the girl from the city who knew how to read and write and could discuss Confucius. I found it hard to blame First Wife for her bad temper.

Imagine that flirtatious girl in the sepia photograph that my cousin Kung kept in his Taishan house. My mother was a young, capable woman who had escaped from an untenable marriage. She found herself in a tiny, isolated village, where no one knew her, and she suddenly realized that this man, my father, was attracted to her. She must have seen this situation as an opening in a life of closing doors and knew that if she played her cards right, the Gold Mountain guest just might be the key to resolving her predicament. I pictured her sitting at the table in my father's house while First Wife served dinner, my mother and father deep into a conversation about books, one that deliberately excluded First Wife. Poor First Wife, seething in the background. I didn't like the way my mother appeared in this story—manipulative and calculating. But I'm not sure I would have behaved any better, given what was at stake.

After my father had his future told, did he share the fortune teller's premonition with my mother right away? Did he tell her about their mutual destiny during one of his many after-school visits? In sharing a revelation from this higher power, he would have implicitly declared his affections for her, even if he had said nothing overt about love. How did my mother receive this news? No one in the village, including my father, would have known that she was married. A woman of her background should have been number one wife, but a secure future was in reach, and she was not about to lose the opportunity just because she was married to that very no-good man.

The villagers must have thought it odd that my mother would be willing to be a *second*. Perhaps they took it as just another indication of the status my father held as a Gold Mountain guest. I pondered my mother's response. From her perspective, being number two to an illiterate woman was better than being forever tied to her first husband, better than being penniless and single, fates that she must have thought almost worse than death. While I was single, my mother worried about me incessantly. Her greatest fear was that I would be a lifetime spinster, that there would be no one to look after me. She never considered that I might be able to look after myself.

Perhaps I was being overly suspicious and unkind. It is possible that my parents had fallen in love and saw the fortune teller's divination as a sign that they were preordained to be together. How much time did they spend discussing this situation, I wondered, before my father approached First Wife? Perhaps he naïvely thought that these two women would live happily together under a single roof. And my mother would have regarded anything as better than life with that very no-good man.

My father may have couched his plan in such a way that his marrying the young teacher would seem to be in the best interests of First Wife. Or he may have presented it as a pronouncement from above, an imperative to be obeyed. Whatever he said, First Wife unleashed her temper, and my father acquiesced to her demands. I found myself puzzled to hear that he wanted her permission, that he didn't ignore her wishes and proceed as he had wanted. Perhaps he just didn't want to deal with her rage. Maybe my father knew that if he returned to North America, he would be leaving my mother, a young woman, alone with an angry older one.

My mother must have been devastated by First Wife's opposition. And her opinion of my father must have suffered when she saw that he could not stand up to his wife. Or perhaps my father never confessed his feelings to my mother and sought a fortune teller without her ever knowing. I doubt it, though. There's only one thing certain: my father cared for my mother. If he hadn't, he would not have gone to a fortune teller or bothered to raise the topic of taking a second wife with First Wife. And my mother, unless she was blind, would have been aware of his attraction to her. Whether his emotions were ever reciprocated or whether my mother manipulated them to her advantage is something I will never know.

My mother always told me that she left my father's village to go to school in Nanking. She was almost boasting, as if to say that life as a teacher in that forsaken village was never a serious consideration. I now see that her words conveyed another partial truth. What had the villagers been whispering about my parents? I would hear this story about my father's visit to the fortune teller and his prophecy several more times from other family members before my stay in Kaiping was over. More than seventy years later they were still talking about my parents. Even if their affair had not been consummated, my mother would have been perceived as the other woman, angling to become my father's second wife. She must have known that she would be the subject of gossip. But my mother was willing to take a chance that those rumours would be quelled once my father gave her a legitimate position in his family. She had cast a spell over this man, but she had also underestimated First Wife.

Whenever my mother whispered about my father's first wife, her voice betrayed a grudge. I can still hear her words in my ear, hushed and confidential. "Yes, she was nice looking and tall, but she was nasty, with a quick temper. Anyone can see why your father was afraid of her."

Jook was right. My mother *did* chase her father.

A few days earlier, Jook had reminded me not for the first time that she was tall because of her mother. She then turned to me with an ever-so-pitying smile on her face and told me that I, sadly, was small because both my parents were short. This time, I could not help smiling myself. But Jook quickly added, as if to cushion the blow but not necessarily diminish her loyalty to her dead mother, "You are lucky that you look like our father. Your mother was smart but not very good looking." This "love triangle" had happened many years ago, but it was still influencing the way my sister behaved toward me.

Once my mother accepted that her plans had failed, she would also have soon concluded that living in the village as a single woman under a cloud of such suspicion would not have been an option. She had to leave the village and must have written to her *thoh*. But would she have told her sister-in-law the real story or would she have contrived another? It now seems to me that the decision to study in Nanking was not a decision, but rather a manoeuvre that would rescue her from another untenable situation. Small wonder that my mother felt so indebted to her *thoh*.

My entire childhood had been spent in dark, tight quarters, where people sniped at each other while placing all their ambitions on me, the one who was able to go to school, to university, to one day live like the *lo fons*, the one who would eventually justify their sacrifices. I thought again about the apartment above the store in Cheong Hong See—that wide staircase and those airy, light-filled, spacious rooms. Never before had I associated my parents with anything beautiful. When my father returned to China in 1947, he'd had no intention of leaving. He was living out what the gods had intended, not just marrying for a second time, but marrying the woman he had fallen in love with many years before. My father must have felt he had finally arrived, that fortune, after so many years of turning away from him, had at last decided to smile in his direction. Were there moments of tenderness in that apartment? It was heartbreaking to contemplate it but just as hard to know what the future held.

My mother's decision to write a letter proposing marriage was a bold, calculated move, one with much potential for failure and humiliation. I had grown up with a certain admiration for this woman who'd looked at her circumstances with steady, dispassionate eyes and arrived at a strategy that would benefit both parties. But in a single afternoon my perception of my parents had changed. When my mother wrote that critical letter proposing marriage, I believe it would have been with the conviction that my father had at one time cared about her and had planned to make her a part of his family. For so long I had seen my mother as a brave, steely woman: her letter, a business proposition written to a man with whom she had once had a professional relationship. But I now realized that she was also an opportunist. She was a woman writing from a position of strength to a man who she knew would not refuse her. And what about her words? Would they have been straightforward or honeyed? In her letter would she have recalled their mutual love of books and history? Would she have reminded him about the fortune teller's prophecy? As my father read her words, he must have thought back with fondness on the times spent with this well-spoken girl who had bestowed so much status on his tiny village and with whom he'd been able to share a love of poetry and philosophy. He must also have been flattered. In all likelihood my father would have felt that there was only one possible course of action. All practical matters aside, marriage to my mother would simply be living out their destiny.

I was quiet on the ride back toward Kaiping City. The scenery that had left me breathless in the morning barely made an impression. The shadows were lengthening, and I knew that it would soon be dusk. I started thinking about a story my cousin Kung had told me during my visit to his home in Taishan. After my mother and her first husband were married, his parents had set them up in a store for selling the produce grown on their farm. They were a family of landowners and successful farmers; my mother should have had a decent life. On one particular occasion, she was away for the day and came back to find the store stripped. Her husband had sold everything: the tables, chairs, cupboards, even the window blinds. He needed the money for white powder. My cousin hesitated for a moment, then said that my mother's first husband had also beaten her. I stared at Kung in disbelief. He looked away and muttered under his breath as if he shouldn't have shared this information with me, as if he had somehow shamed the memory of my mother. "I don't know for sure . . . but that's what my mother told me," my cousin mumbled.

Mo vun fut. Mo vun fut. What choice did I have? I can still hear my mother's voice—sometimes a plea for sympathy, sometimes a bitter statement full of resentment. How terrible must it have been for her to have to go back to that very no-good man during the war. So this was why it would have been acceptable to be a second to my father's illiterate first wife. At least my father was kind, decent and responsible.

During a visit to my mother's nursing home, toward the end of her life, I found her lying in bed, facing the wall and wailing, "Wwwhy? Look at her! She's *lum lum, huk huk*, blue, blue, black black. She's dead! My daughter is dead. You've beaten and kicked her to death." I called out to her, telling her that I was alive and standing next to her bed. My mother's body stiffened and she slowly turned to look at me. Her face was frozen with shock and fear. I reached over and stroked her cheek. She took my hand in hers, her features softening with relief, her eyes welling with tears. "I thought you were dead," she whispered. "Somebody told me that Michael had beaten you to death." A wave of anger flooded through my body. How could she say this about her son-in-law, my husband who had welcomed her into our home, who cooked her favourite meals, who was often a personal chauffeur, who had been generous and accommodating. But I said nothing except to reassure her that I was very much alive and well. I had to remind myself that my mother had dementia and not to take her mumblings seriously. But after hearing my cousin, I saw things from a new perspective: in her delusion it wasn't me who was being beaten. It was my mother herself. Now I understood why she took the chances she did in that tiny village and why she deceived my father over a decade later when she wrote that fateful proposal of marriage. She was desperate to be rescued.

Whenever I think about these events, I see in my mind my mother, sobbing with grief, at my father's funeral. I can remember my surprise at the depth of her emotional response to the death of a man she had never seemed to love. Perhaps I'd had it right when I was a child. Perhaps my mother and Ming Nee did greet my father with joy and jubilation when he got off the boat. And when they rode the sedan chair back to the village, their laughter filled the air, certain the stars had finally brought them together and placed before them a bright, happy future.

We were approaching the outskirts of Kaiping City. The day's excursion had left everyone fatigued and me distracted. But my nieces insisted on stopping at their brother's orange grove. Kim said it was not far from the main road and should take us no more than an hour or so out of our way. I hesitated, but Michael reminded me that we were being offered an opportunity to see a side of the country that would not be available to the average tourist. He was right.

We had seen very little of my nephew Chong on this trip because he was busy with his orange grove. He lived in Kaiping City and rode his motorcycle to his farm every day. Kim directed our driver down another stony, deeply rutted trail, but it couldn't get all the way into the orchard, so we left it parked and walked the rest of the way. Once we departed from the trail, the six of us continued single file down a winding dirt path until we arrived at a hillside covered with orange trees that were laden with plump, round fruit. We came to a small clearing and found my nephew with his workers, building a new dormitory. When he saw us, he left his workers and took us on a tour of his orchard.

Along the way, Kim showed us where she had cultivated plantings of ginger and *muk see*, a large, yam-like root. She went into a storage shed and returned with a hoe. Lifting the tool above her shoulder, she brought it down with a single, forceful chop. The *muk see* bush that had been over six feet tall, with several robust stalks, was now severed and lying on its side. My husband glanced at me, his eyes wide with admiration. Kim then loosened the earth around the *muk see*, and we all bent over and helped her harvest the crop.

The stems of the ginger plant were delicate and no more than eighteen inches long, and its leaves were narrow and grass-like. The roots, when dug from the earth, were pale and fat, so much more succulent than anything I'd ever seen in a grocery store back home. I watched my nieces chatting and laughing as they worked, and I found myself wondering whether I would have been like them if my mother and I had stayed in China. It was hard not to admire these two women. They were both assured and capable. Although Kim's formal education had been sabotaged, her life was rich, helping various family members, visiting with her brothers, haggling in the markets. Her cell phone rang frequently with calls from friends. I looked at Su and saw my mother. If she had been able to finish her studies in silkworm culture, she would have been like this, an independent woman with her own store. I could picture her unravelling bolts of gorgeous silk for interested customers, helping them decide which one to purchase.

Chong picked some of the ripest oranges from his trees and passed them around to all of us. Michael wanted to see the entire property, so my nephew led us on a walk along a path that I suspected would take us to the end of the grove. To my amazement, at the boundary of Chong's farm, there was another hill with more cultivated fields, and just beyond that was a collection of old, tumbledown buildings, a tucked-in-the-corner hamlet. "This country is *so* old," said Michael. "You get the sense that there's no such thing as the *end of the trail*. You can go down the most obscure, overgrown path that should lead nowhere and suddenly you're looking at something: a small holding, a cluster of buildings, an out-of-the-way village."

The sky was thinly streaked with clouds, and the light was still warm and soft—on the cusp of darkness. We stood for another few minutes, then started to retrace our footsteps. By the time we got back to the van, I could see the moon, like a giant orange itself, glowing against a darkening sky. It seemed so close I felt I could reach up and pluck it.

※

One of my strongest childhood memories is of my mother sleeping. Whenever there was a break from work, she chose to lie down. It wasn't until I was an adult that I realized the obvious: she was depressed. My relatives in China saw my parents almost as mythic characters. I so wished I could share their point of view, but to me they were testaments to self-denial and endurance. Other families produced heroes who performed fantastic feats, prevailing against all odds. With my parents there were no fantastic feats. With them it was never what they gave me; it was what they gave up. I could not brag about lessons, tuition for camp, an airline ticket or help with a down payment for a home. When I try to describe their gifts, words fail me.

The story of my family is filled with ghosts, their presence resonating from beyond the grave. In the course of a year, their whispers have turned my doubt and arrogance into a richer sort of knowing, and I have watched my parents grow into fully fleshed human beings. At the same time they have also turned into strangers. The more I find out about them, the further they are removed from the people who eked out a living in a small-town hand laundry. I cannot connect this charming, much-admired and respected woman to my sharp-tongued mother, consumed by bitterness. I cannot connect this confident man with high standing in his community to the diminished man whom I knew as my father, to the man who ended his life at the end of a rope. My parents were unhappy exiles in the Gold Mountain, shadows of their former selves. I am left aching to know the man and the woman who knew each other before I was born. Whatever truth I now hold feels insignificant and false.

TWENTY-TWO

My sister Jook lived with her son Liang and his family in the village of Ong Sun, where Su also had her herbal pharmacy. The morning after our trip to Ai Sah and Yellow Olive, we met Kim at the Kaiping bus station and boarded the 10 a.m. bus to Ong Sun for a last visit with my sister. We would also see Liang and his farm, which was on the outskirts of the village. In another few days, we'd be leaving for Shanghai.

As we headed out of town, the bus stopped every few blocks to let on other riders, each paying with a handful of soiled-looking bills. But before arriving at Ong Sun, Kim wanted to stop and show us her husband's ancestral village, which was on the same road. As it turned out, it was only a few hundred yards from Ning Kai Lee. This made sense. Kim's married name was Fong, and the cluster of villages in this area was all inhabited by Fongs. The village resembled my father's, but it was in much worse shape. At one time it had been home to forty households with a population of about two hundred people. Now, only four households with about twenty people still lived there. Kim led us to her husband's ancestral house and unlocked the door. The air was stale, and I could smell the dampness in the bricks. Black mildew was growing on some of the surfaces. It had not been occupied for almost fifteen years. In one room I saw sheets of paper glued to the wall. It was hard to tell what was on them because they were discoloured and wrinkled with moisture. But on closer inspection, I could see that the pictures were of glamorous young women dressed in fashionable clothes, pictures of Chinese movie and singing stars, clipped from magazines. Kim smiled and told me that her daughter, who now lived in Ottawa, had pasted them there when she was a teenager.

Several weeks before coming to China, Michael and I had driven to Ottawa and met Kim's daughter for the first time. While we were there, Michael took dozens of pictures of her, her husband, her baby and their new, suburban house. When I gave these photos to Kim, there was pleasure and longing on her face, and she poured out questions about her daughter and grandchild. I felt both pleased and guilty. It was unfair that she was unable to visit her daughter and granddaughter while I had the resources to hop on a plane to China for a holiday. I looked at the posters of those women in typical movie star poses, hair coiffed and smiles perfect, eyes flirting with the camera. Kim's daughter, in some ways, had been like her great-grandfather, my father—fantasizing about the Gold Mountain.

A few days before, Kim and I had sat together in the garden across the road from the Ever Joint Hotel. We'd been shopping in downtown Kaiping and decided to rest for a while before I returned to my room. She told me once again that she and her husband wanted to emigrate and join their daughter overseas. Her daughter was in the process of sponsoring them, and they hoped to go in another two years. She was worried, though, about passing the interview with the immigration officers. She had heard rumours about a trained cook who'd given the wrong answer for preparing a fish and was subsequently refused entry. I said this was unlikely, since Canada had a point system and that if the applicant was refused, it was most likely because he didn't have a high enough score. Kim nodded politely. I could tell she doubted my response.

As my niece spoke about her desire to live overseas, I thought about my mother and how she never adjusted to her new country. She'd arrived in her early forties, and if Kim were to immigrate she would be doing so in her sixties. The last time my niece spoke to me about her desire to emigrate, I'd kept my opinion to myself. But now I wanted to tell her that although she'd be living with her daughter in a comfortable house in the suburbs, homes in Canada were not like homes in southern China—friendly to the outdoors, welcoming to friends dropping by. I wanted to tell her that she'd have to depend on others for transportation, that she'd be far away from Chinatown, that she wouldn't be able to talk to friends on her cell phone, that she wouldn't be able to haggle in the markets, that she would no longer harvest fresh ginger from her brother's farm or help at her sister's tidy herbal pharmacy. I wanted to warn her that winters in Ottawa were cold beyond her comprehension. I knew how much Kim missed her daughter and longed to see her granddaughter, and I suppose she also longed for what she saw as my wealth and comfortable lifestyle. But Canada was my home, and English was my language.

Kim was my niece, but our friendship was new and I did not know her well. There was so much I wanted to tell her. But, it was not my place. I told her to think carefully before she left her rich, independent life in China.

By the time we got back on the bus and arrived at the Ong Sun station, it was early afternoon. I had barely stepped onto the street when a motorcycle taxi, trying to hustle customers, came so close he almost ran me over. Jook had been standing nearby with her neck craned, watching for us to disembark. She rushed over and scolded the taxi driver.

It was market day, and on the way to my nephew's home, Jook led us past a variety of outdoor stalls, selling everything from live chickens to "Jackie Chan" condoms. As usual, people would stop whatever they were doing to gawk at us.

Two teenaged school girls started to follow us, visibly curious about Michael. When we stopped in front of a fruit stall, Michael smiled at them and said, "Hello." This friendly gesture encouraged the girls to finally approach us. They spoke to Michael in their halting English and asked to have their picture taken with him. They gave their phone numbers to Kim, and we promised to mail her copies of the photo once we arrived home. By this time a small crowd had gathered around us. My sister was chuckling and announced to the onlookers that I was her *moi*, her little sister, and that my husband and I had returned from the Gold Mountain.

My sister linked her arm through mine, and we continued our happy stroll through the market. Jook smiled and waved at her friends. She had lived in Ong Sun for almost sixty years and knew most of the villagers. She wanted everyone to know that I had come halfway around the world to visit her.

We walked past a table display of seeds in paper envelopes with pictures of bok choy, gai lan, bitter melon, fuzzy melon and winter melon, all vegetables my father had grown in his garden. The vendor smiled at us and tried to convince us to buy, but we could buy seeds like these at home. Then, just as we were about to leave, my husband saw a package of *dow mew*, seeds for green pea shoots. We had routinely eaten these shoots in Chinatown restaurants, but Michael had been unable to find seeds to grow them himself. He picked up the package and started to turn it over, even though he couldn't read the Chinese script. The vendor told us they were a superior variety. As soon as he gave us a price, my sister reminded him that she lived in the village and that she would not let him overcharge her brother-in-law just because he was from the Gold Mountain. The man laughed and offered a lower price. My sister nodded begrudging approval. I was sure we could find the seeds at a Chinese nursery back home, but they often sold their goods in packages without pictures, and I couldn't read the Chinese characters. Besides, my spoken Cantonese was inadequate. I chuckled to myself as Michael paid the vendor. We had our seeds, even though we'd come all the way to China to find them.

After a short stop at Su's herbal pharmacy, we walked to Liang's house, which is completely open to the street. The edge of his living room borders the sidewalk, and people can step in and out of his house without going through a door. Instead, a roll-up gate, much like a garage door, closes the house at night. While we sat drinking tea, a boy who was probably ten or eleven walked into the room. He stood for a few moments and stared at me and Michael. When I asked my nephew who the boy was, he answered that he didn't know. *You don't know?* I thought to myself. Who did this child think he was, walking into somebody's house without being invited? I remember once being told that there is no word in Chinese for privacy. Privacy as I know it seems to be a Western concept. The boy remained for several minutes while my relatives carried on with their conversation and after a few more minutes he left.

Houses in Canada seal off the elements, but they also seal in their inhabitants. After living in homes where the line between outdoor and indoor was nearly imperceptible, had my parents found that those northern houses added to their isolation?

266

My nephew Liang works his land with a vehicle called a *gow-gung char*, which translates into "dog-work cart," a small tractor with handlebars instead of a steering wheel. He told us to get into the wagon hitched to the back and drove us along a dirt road so rough that if I hadn't hung onto the edge of the wagon, I would have fallen out. Once we arrived at his fields, we got out and walked along dirt paths and over narrow bridges, past fish ponds and a reforested area alive with butterflies. We crossed a high cement bridge over a stream and saw a derelict stone mill, a mill pond and a dam far below. Farther down the stream, two men were fishing. One was using a long, bamboo rod to propel a raft made from a large slab of Styrofoam, while the man at the front held a long, wooden pole attached to a metal rod wired to a large battery. His other hand gripped the handle of a small net. As he put the metal rod in the water, he activated an electrical current, making a musical whirr. Stunned fish would float to the surface, and he would scoop them up with the net. Michael and I watched this ingenious process for several minutes. I then remembered that on our walk up the mountain in Ai Sah, we had run across a toad catcher who was using an electrical rod in the same way. Once again, our fascination with such commonplace things amused my relatives.

Liang pointed out which of the fields around us belonged to him; they were close to each other, but not all adjacent. I marvelled that his farm is productive twelve months of the year. He grows rice, sugar cane, bananas, lychees and garden vegetables and raises pigs, chickens, ducks and fish. The fertility of the Pearl Delta never ceased to amaze me.

After our tour Michael and I spent the afternoon sitting under a lychee tree, eating bananas that Kim and Liang's wife had harvested earlier that afternoon. I pointed to some mountains in the distance and was told that they were named for their shapes: Cow Mountain, Horse Mountain and Goose Mountain. When it was time for dinner, my nephew and his neighbour each held an end of a long fishnet, and by pulling it through his pond caught two large fish. Liang's wife picked vegetables and dug up some ginger root, and Kim caught a duck. Holding the duck with both wings behind its back, she bent back its neck so its wings and head could be gripped in one hand. With her feet apart and her knees slightly bent, my niece looked like a performer in a martial arts movie. She took up a cleaver in her other hand and in one swift, fluid motion, she slit the bird's throat. Kim then held the duck upside down as the blood dripped slowly onto the ground.

Every Saturday while I was growing up in Acton, a farmer delivered a chicken inside a brown burlap bag. My father then kept the unsuspecting fowl inside the drying room behind the kitchen for the night. On Sunday he would catch it, slit its throat and hold it over a bowl to collect the dripping blood, which my mother would later steam into a pudding. He had figured out that this should not be done in our backyard, where the neighbours would witness what they might consider to be a primitive slaughter. One weekend my father ordered two chickens, and when they'd both been plucked and cleaned, he wrapped one of them in brown laundry paper and told me to take it to a neighbour who had been especially kind to us. I did as instructed in spite of being deeply embarrassed by what I thought was a most inappropriate gift. A few days later, when I saw our neighbour in a store on the main street of Acton, I tried to sneak past her. But she saw me and told me that my father's chicken was the best she'd ever had. I wanted to get away as fast as I could, but she insisted on talking and made me promise to thank my father for her.

The table was spread with food from my nephew's farm. Kim had steamed the duck with hoisin sauce and slices of *muk see*, the yam-like root. Liang's wife had fried the fish whole, so the skin was brown and crispy, then smothered it with garlic and ginger. Early in the afternoon, Su had started making a medicinal soup of berries and roots simmered in chicken broth. "We don't have much money," my nephew said, "but we always have lots to eat."

With a broad grin across her face, his wife added, "Today we have lots of money. We sold two hundred yuans' worth of bananas at the market!"

Partway through dinner, Liang invited us to spend the night at his house. He had extra beds. I was touched by his hospitality but ended up declining, saying that we'd already paid for the hotel room. But that was not the only reason. Earlier in the afternoon, I'd been in their bathroom, where I'd seen the wooden tub and ladle. Even though I'd camped and canoed in the Canadian outdoors, I could not face using the washing facilities in that home. I felt terrible turning down my nephew's offer because my reaction was so irrational. But that basin and ladle reminded me too much of bathing in my father's laundry, crouching inside a wooden laundry tub next to an enamel basin of warm water, rinsing the soap off my skinny, shivering body with a wet cloth.

Later, Liang's wife brought out a photo album of her daughter's wedding. My sister told me to sit beside her on the wooden sofa. They were eager for Michael and me to see pictures of this auspicious family occasion. The album was full of studio photographs of the bride and groom in wedding clothes and in fairytale-like ball gowns and tuxedos, all taken against a backdrop of painted formal gardens. This wedding in rural Kaiping wasn't all that different from what I knew in Canada: a single day of living out a fantasy. But what struck me were the group photos. Everyone, even the parents of the couple being married, was dressed in everyday clothes. Kim was actually now wearing what she'd had on that day. It suddenly occurred to me that even though I'd been with Kim almost every day for the month we'd been in Kaiping, I'd seen her in only two different shirts. And here I was living out of a suitcase and still in a different outfit each day of the week.

Liang's wife closed the album and Jook said, "When I got married, I was only seventeen and I hadn't even met my husband. On my wedding day, I wore a veil so thick I couldn't see through it. At the end of the day, when it was lifted, I saw three men in the room and I didn't even know which one I'd married!" Everyone giggled. My sister sighed and shook her head, "*Tsk*, how could I possibly know? We'd never laid eyes on each other. Then somebody, probably my mother-in-law, led us both into a bedroom. We were both still children, didn't know anything. We were so frightened. I spent the night on the bed, and he slept on the floor." My sister sighed.

"Of all my brothers and sisters, my life has been the worst. You can't imagine how many tears I've shed. If only my mother hadn't been so stubborn. If she'd allowed Father to marry your mother, she might have lived."

"You think she should have listened to the fortune teller?" I said.

My sister shook her head. "You haven't heard everything. You spent your life in the Gold Mountain. Lucky." My sister paused. Just as Michael had said, in China there was no such thing as the end of a trail.

"Mother had a terrible temper. After Father told her about the fortune teller saying he was fated to have two wives and that her life depended on a second wife coming into the family, she threw a tantrum. Father could not convince her to allow a second. In the end he gave in, but he shouldn't have. Your mother was in the village for only two or three years, and then she left for Nanking to go to school. I think Mother was really relieved to see her go. Father went back to Canada in 1937. When he left I was only six years old, and when he came back, I was seventeen, and within a few months

I was married. I barely knew him. But then I have no real memory of Mother. Father was gone for not even three years and she was dead. When I look back, as far as Mother was concerned, the fortune teller was wrong. Here it was years after the prediction and she was still alive. Her life didn't depend on a second wife."

I'd heard this story already. How many more times would I have to listen to it before leaving China? I was about to say something but then decided against it. Jook was my older sister, and it would have been disrespectful of me to interrupt.

"The year that Shing was ten, I was nine and Doon was four, she took us to spend Chinese New Year with her brother. Mother was in a good mood. She was alive and healthy, proof that the fortune teller was wrong. She was right not to let that little button of a city girl into her house. So what if she couldn't read and write; she was number one wife. There was no need for a second. That was what Mother said over and over. And with my father regularly sending money back, we were doing well.

"We were all looking forward to going back to Mother's home village, and my uncle knew that his sister had a special fondness for dog meat stew. He had gone to a lot of trouble and had made the stew the night before. Everyone knows that the best dog stew is overnight dog stew. That way the meat has a chance to become more tender and to absorb the flavour of the other ingredients. Well, Mother must have found the dish really tasty because she ate too much and ended up with indigestion. When we went home, one of the villagers told her that the stew had too much yang and that she needed something to cool her body, something that was mostly yin. Mother made herself a sweet soup from yellow beans. But she didn't know that dog meat and yellow beans were very bad together, that the juices from the meat would cause the beans to expand and explode. I sat up all night with her. Mother died in terrible pain. I can still see her writhing and hear her screams. So the fortune teller was right after all. Her prediction came true, and my father did end up with two wives. If only Mother had listened, then she might have lived and we would not have been orphaned.

"Those years after Mother died were terrible, and when the Japanese closed off the seaports, conditions got worse. When she was alive Father sent the money to her, of course, but after she died he sent the money to First Brother. He'd been married for just a few months and at first he looked after us, but then he started to gamble and we were left to starve. His bride was only seventeen, not at all ready to look after three children. And when she got pregnant later that year, she was so fed up that she went back to live with her mother. The three of us were left on our own." My sister shook her head and wagged her finger at me. "Of all Father's children, you are the luckiest."

I nodded in silent agreement, not knowing what to say. I was seated between my niece, who was the same age as me, and my sister, who was old enough to be my mother. The gulf between us felt as wide as the Pacific.

❧

273

Jook and I held each other for a long time. She was staying in Ong Sun, and Michael and I would leave Kaiping in another day. Little did I know that this would be the last time I would see my sister. She would die from a stroke the following year. My brothers would each send a large amount of money back to China for her hospital care and then for funeral expenses.

When I spoke to Shing about the money, he said that he and Doon wanted to honour Jook's memory. He reminded me once again that after their mother had died, it was Jook who cared for them, who scavenged the food, cooked it and kept them alive. "She was our only sister," Shing said to me. His statement startled me. I almost blurted out, *What about me? I'm your sister. Don't I count?* But in that moment I understood that I had not been a part of their childhood. And so I didn't play a role in their grief. My brother's words revealed just how much the three of them had remained bound by those early experiences, the sadness of all those years apart adding to the depth of their loss.

"I'm so glad we all went back to China," I said. It was all I could offer to comfort my grieving brother.

Kim, Michael and I hurried to catch the bus back to Kaiping City. A throng of motorcycle taxis had gathered at the bus stop and their drivers were offering to take us directly to our hotel. Our relatives all thought this would be a good idea because we'd save on the taxi fare from the bus station in

Kaiping City. But Michael and I both declined without even consulting each other. The driving in China made me nervous even during the day, but to be a passenger on a motorcycle at night when drivers often didn't bother to turn on their headlights wasn't even a consideration.

Once the bus arrived, we weren't allowed to board but were told to stand aside and wait until the inside was cleaned. We watched the female attendant sweep the debris from under the seats and the aisle onto the sidewalk, where it stayed.

There were no lights on the road back to Kaiping City. People flagged the bus down at random, and even though it was hard to distinguish landmarks in the night, passengers always seemed to know where to get off. In spite of these distractions, I couldn't stop thinking about what my sister had told me. Only a few days before, I'd naïvely thought that I finally had all the facts about my parents' lives here in China. But the story of First Wife's death had changed all that. It lingered with me during the entire ride back.

From a Western perspective, there was something particularly horrible about dying from eating the flesh of a dog. The thought of it made my stomach churn. Was she in the loft of my father's house or would they have brought her down to the family living area? First Brother and his wife would have been ministering to her. They would likely have asked for help from a woman in the village who was known for her healing abilities. In a tiny village like Ning Kai Lee, there wouldn't have been a doctor. Perhaps other neighbours had gathered around her bedside. And what about the three children? I kept thinking about them and how frightened they must have been, watching their mother writhe in pain, listening to her piercing screams. Was she gripped with terror for her own children and what the future held for them? With their father stranded on the other side of the world, they were, in fact, orphaned.

Listening to my sister during this visit, as far as she was concerned, she might as well not have had a father. When he finally returned to China after the war, it was to marry my mother, and a few months later, Jook, being of marriageable age, would become the wife of a man she'd never met. One of my nieces whispered to me that the villagers gossiped about Jook's dowry being somewhat modest, bearing in mind that her father was a Gold Mountain guest. People said it was my mother's fault. If First Wife had been alive, she would have made sure that her daughter left home with a large dowry. No one seemed to blame my father. It was a woman's responsibility, so they blamed my mother. I found this village gossip difficult to fathom; my mother's generosity with these people had been legendary. She'd probably had no experience assembling a dowry and didn't know how much to give. It was the only criticism I heard about my mother.

We were back in our hotel room, drinking tea and writing in our journals. I told Michael again about First Wife's unhappy end at the hand of the gods. He put down his pen and shrugged. "It's all very sad. But it probably had nothing to do with the gods," said my agnostic husband. "My hunch is that it was either appendicitis or food poisoning. I'd say appendicitis. If it had been food poisoning, more people would have been sick. The mix of dog meat and yellow beans had nothing to do with it. Just makes for a good story."

I agreed with my husband. He was being rational and so very Western. And yet, when my sister told me about the death of her mother, my spine tingled. To her and to some other members of my family, it was as fate had intended. Once her wilful mother had chosen to defy the gods, she was doomed. Her father was preordained to have two wives, and if First Wife would not cooperate, the gods themselves had no choice but to engineer her death, thus making way for wife number two. If it was indeed predetermined, the gods impressed me as being especially cruel and merciless. I felt sorry for this peasant woman, whose only crime was not wanting to share her husband with another wife. As these thoughts drifted through my mind, I found myself contemplating the real reason why my mother returned to our ancestral home before leaving for Hong Kong and then the Gold Mountain. Once again, I could see the wheels of the pedicab spinning over a bumpy path and I remembered the softness of my mother's body as she held me on her lap. I have no doubt that she was returning to request the blessing of our ancestors, but perhaps even more important, she was surely attempting to make peace with the spirit of First Wife.

TWENTY-THREE

My father had finally sold the laundry in Acton and with the proceeds, my parents bought a shoebox of a house, a tiny row house on a short, secluded street in Toronto's Chinatown, not far from Dundas Street. Like so many Chinese of their generation, they kept a room for themselves and rented out the rest. My mother was dividing her time between my father in Toronto and helping my brother at his restaurant an hour or so outside the city. She and my father were far from happy, but at least they seemed to have reached a truce. The terrible quarrels that used to consume them and terrify me as a child were now a thing of the past.

Shing had a steady job with Canada Post, and Doon owned a restaurant with a solid business. Ming Nee had married a university professor and was living a comfortable life in a large, suburban house. They all had children. I had a real job, having graduated from university the year before with a liberal arts degree. My parents had hoped I would enter one of the higher-level professions such as law or medicine, but I had neither the interest nor the academic inclination.

Nevertheless, I was the first person in my immediate family to finish university, and my parents were proud of that. On the day of my convocation, my parents were in the audience, and as I walked across the stage to receive my degree, I saw my father lift his peaked cap in recognition.

I remembered thinking that being an assistant at the Ontario College of Art library was a pretty special position to have landed. I was a small town girl, and the fact that they had chosen me above the other applicants had been a personal triumph. My parents were proud that I was financially independent at such an early age, and my mother bragged to her friends that I was sharing an apartment with some other girls and that her daughter had an annual salary of over five thousand dollars! "Not bad for a girl," one of them said. My father told me many times how happy he was that I was making a living using my head and not my hands. Even with my modest income, I had comforts that my parents only dreamed about in their Gold Mountain life. I was on my way to living like a *lo fon*.

༈

In the short walk from the Ontario College of Art to my parents' house, my clothes had become damp. We were in the middle of a July heat wave. Even breathing required effort. My mother had returned to the city the day before and had invited me to have lunch with her and my father.

The moment she opened the front door of their little row house, I knew she'd spent the morning cooking. Her forehead was shiny with perspiration. I could smell garlic and the distinctive aroma of long-simmering soup. I saw the dishes on the kitchen table: four-flavour soup from pork bones, almond seeds, lily bulbs, lotus seeds and red dates; steamed fish; and stir-fried green beans with fermented tofu. My mother had gone to a lot of trouble; she was constantly worried about what I ate. I gave my parents each a hug and sat down, resigned to eating the hot food my mother had made with such love and concern, when all I wanted was a salad. My father appeared particularly haggard that day. He was wearing a thin, white T-shirt instead of his usual white button-up shirt with rolled-up sleeves. I thought his breathing seemed laboured. In spite of my lack of hunger, I ate a whole bowl of rice and drank a full bowl of soup. It was delicious. I was just about finished when my father reached across the table with his chopsticks and accidentally knocked over his soup.

"*Eeiyah*, look how clumsy you are," my mother scolded. "Can't do anything right."

My father sat there, defeated, unable to say a single word.

"Never mind, never mind," I said, trying to smooth things over.

I helped her tidy the mess, and whatever friction there was between them seemed to dissipate. They both smiled and waved goodbye at the door. But I didn't want to leave. Even though a certain equilibrium had been restored, I saw the exhaustion in my father's face. His chest looked hollow under his shapeless T-shirt, and his mouth was slack. His breathing was so shallow I could almost feel the effort behind it. All the way back to the college library, I kept seeing his face.

My mother had never before phoned me at work. But shortly after my return, when a co-worker handed me the telephone, I knew without even being told, that it was my mother. I knew she was calling about my father. My mother told me in a strangled voice that my father was dead. "Hurry. Come. Hurry. Come. Now," she said between gasps of breath. I felt dizzy with fear.

I ran the few blocks that separated the College of Art from my parents' house. The sun hurt my eyes; my shirt was sodden and stuck to my skin. My chest felt like a hollow cave, my heart pounding against the walls. When I arrived neighbours were crowded around an ambulance parked outside the house. The back doors were open, and a couple of paramedics were sliding in a stretcher with a body draped from head to toe in a white sheet. My mother was standing a little to the side with her hands pressed against her mouth. Her face was ashen. When I put my arms around her, she let out a long, painful moan. Her body crumpled and I could barely hold her up. At the same time her fingers dug into my shoulders. Everyone was watching us. Nobody said a word. This couldn't be happening to us. That couldn't really be my father on the stretcher. But it was. We stood clinging to each other, sobbing, afraid to let go.

Long after I'd led her back into the house, my mother continued crying, stopping only to catch her breath. Those last moments with my father emerged from her in reluctant fragments. But finally I was able to piece together what had happened. After I had left to return to work, my father went into the basement while my mother stayed in the kitchen doing the dishes. She heard something clatter to the floor. For some reason she knew that things were not right and ran down the stairs, not even bothering to dry her hands. There was my father with a rope around his neck, dangling from a beam in the ceiling. She rushed over and wrapped her arms around his legs, pushing him up, trying to ease the pressure of the rope. He still felt warm, but it was too late.

The following few days were a blur. The same village uncle who had greeted my mother and me at the airport when we'd arrived in Canada almost twenty years earlier now accompanied me to one of the Chinese newspapers and wrote the obituary. Afterwards, he took me to a restaurant where we booked a post-funeral reception. My brother Shing and I went to the local funeral home and chose a coffin. We picked an oak casket that cost seven hundred dollars. I purchased a double plot at Mount Pleasant cemetery and helped my brother choose a pink granite headstone. My brother wrote in Chinese characters on a sheet of paper for the stone carver my father's dates and that he was a native of Ning Kai Lee, Kaiping County, Guangdong Province, China.

At twenty-two years old, I was the youngest child in our family but not too young to supervise the arrangements at a funeral home in Chinatown where only English was spoken.

Shing, Doon, Ming Nee and their spouses and people who were distantly related through our ancestral village were at the funeral. A friend I had known since high school was there with her aunt. Michael sat with them. So much of that day remains a blur, except for my mother and how inconsolable she was. Even now, when I think about the lack of affection in their marriage, the depth of her sorrow seems out of proportion. It didn't seem to matter whether she was standing or sitting; her body was crippled with grief. Every time I glanced at her, she was bent over, unable to straighten herself. All the mourners voiced their shock in a constant refrain. His children were all doing so well. He had so much to be proud of. He was an old man already. Why did he end his life like that?

I stayed with my mother for a couple of weeks after my father's death. She'd already decided she wouldn't continue to live in the row house. Within a week of my father's death, all the tenants had moved, our home tainted by suicide. She decided that she'd no longer let out rooms but would rent the entire house to a non-Chinese family instead. I was expected to find the tenants, to collect the rent and look after her house. She would now live with Doon's family in the apartment above his restaurant.

At one point I asked if she was afraid to sleep in the house, and she replied that there was nothing to fear. "Your father died a terrible death. But your father was a good man," she said to me. "He would never do harm to you, me or anyone. You must never forget that."

I felt my mother's strength returning in her words, and yet a few days later, the calm evaporated. I returned from work one evening to find that she'd thrown away all of my father's possessions. Her forehead was beaded with perspiration. She shook with anger, spitting out her words between gasps of breath. She insisted that she'd had to get rid of everything. After he died I remembered seeing the hand-sewn books made from sheets of brown paper, filled with his poetry. I had made a mental note to save them. I had told myself that in time I would find someone to translate the words into English. These books represented a side of my father that had been inaccessible, but I had dreamed that one day it would be revealed to me. Now they were gone, taken away with the trash.

As I looked around the rooms, my jaw went slack and I glared at her. Her feelings about her dead husband swung from grief and despair to uncontrollable rage. I could picture her tearing through his few possessions, throwing them into a green garbage bag. My mother even tossed out his gold watch and fob. For a man who lived without luxury, these were the only things he'd ever owned that were beautiful and hinted at personal indulgence. He'd bought them on his last journey to China and had tucked them inside his waistcoat when coming back to Canada. He used to let me hold the watch, its surface hard and smooth against my fingers. And when I snapped open the small, round door, it revealed a clock face with tiny black numbers. One day it will be yours, he said. The only thing I found that had missed my mother's frenzy was an abacus. I can still see my father sitting at the ironing table, late into the night, adding up the money that he had taken in and subtracting the cost of supplies. I can see his hand poised over the rungs, hear the click-clack of the beads as his fingers pushed them up and down.

I continued to glare at my mother in this half-empty room. *How dare you? How dare you toss out these things? The decisions are not yours alone to make. These things belonged to my father and as his daughter I had a right to them.* I felt rage deep in my gut, surging and rising, filling my lungs. I wanted to open my mouth and scream. Instead, I swallowed and forced everything back, deep inside my belly. It would have been spiteful of me to say anything. But as hard as I tried to keep that anger suppressed, in the years that followed my father's death, every so often it would find a crack in the armour that I had fitted around my resentment, and when it seeped through, the results were hurtful and unsettling. I lashed out over inconsequential things that made me feel mean and ungenerous. The real issue I kept buried, unable to look it in the face. The memory of my mother's shame mingled with anger and sadness will always be with me.

❦

My father's suicide left us, his children and grandchildren, a bitter legacy. More than thirty-five years have passed, and even though we are living good lives, his death haunts us like a dark shadow. Until now I have been unable to speak openly about it. If asked how my father died, I had a ready response.

He was eighty years old, I would say, worn out from all those years of hard work. It was an acceptable reply, one that invited no further queries, one that allowed me to once again bury the dull ache rising in my chest.

Hardly a single day goes by without my thinking of my father and his suicide. For the most part these thoughts are fleeting, but sometimes they refuse to be pushed aside and chill me to the core. The word *why* rings in my head. I can still see him, the way he looked at that last lunch, a man eaten away by despair and humiliation. After I left their house, did my parents pick up their quarrelling? Was his final act a moment of selfish impulsiveness? An extension of that long-ago threat to remove his tongue? Or was it simply that his will to go on was exhausted. I can hear him still, after a fight with my mother, after an interminable day of ironing *lo fon* shirts, washing *lo fon* clothes, his voice dripping with bitterness, muttering to himself. *This* gow meng, *this dog life, this worthless* gow meng.

My father was an old man when he fitted that rope around his neck. Why could he not give us the gift of a peaceful ending? Was this his only way of making sure he would be remembered? Were we, his wife, his children, in some way culpable? I cannot forget my mother at his funeral, grief-stricken. Was she thinking of their unhappy life together, their inability to reach out and comfort each other? Had she said something unforgivable to him on the day of his death? Or was it even deeper? Now that I've heard these stories about them when they first met, I cannot help but wonder if, for a short time, there was a moment when the future held promise, when they might have been in love. At my father's funeral, what was my mother really crying about? how love, transformed into contempt, had poisoned and wasted their lives? These unanswerable questions . . . These sad, unanswerable questions . . .

TWENTY-FOUR

Miss Wong, our young, attractive travel agent, wore an unusual and rather garish top with her blue jeans. During our previous meetings at the Kaiping travel office, she had dressed in a style not unlike that of young women in the West. But today I found it hard not to be distracted by this dark red, silky tank top and her lacy, cream-coloured overblouse, which together created a garment that was halfway between lingerie and an ornate lampshade. But with Miss Wong's help, Michael and I reserved an overnight train to Shanghai from Guangzhou and accommodation in Shanghai, Suzhou, Nanjing and Hangzhou. We'd be leaving the next day.

It was plain that Miss Wong and another young woman did all the work in that small office, while an older, but not yet middle-aged man (whom I presumed to be her boss) spent most of his time talking on the phone. By the time we'd completed our arrangements, Boss Man had put down the telephone receiver. He wished us a pleasant journey, then asked where we were going. I listed the cities and told him that before the war, my mother had been to Nanking to attend school. Boss Man had been listening politely, but with the mention of studies in Nanking, his curiosity was suddenly piqued. He said that my mother must have been very smart to have pursued education in Nanking and that it was still regarded as a major centre of scholarship. Seventy years later and people were still impressed. My mother would have been pleased that I was basking in her former glory.

My mother always referred to the quilted jackets that Chinese people wore as being stuffed with *min*. Our final family dinner in Kaiping was at a restaurant called *Hong Min*, Red Kapok, and when Kim saw me looking at a picture of the kapok flower and seed on the wall, she confirmed my thoughts and told me that the filling for traditional Chinese jackets and quilts was made from the fluffy white down inside the seed pod of this plant. The *Hong Min* was her favourite restaurant, and when Michael and I said we wanted to host a farewell dinner, she suggested that we rent a private room with a TV at the Red Kapok. I had come to rely on Kim and Bing for so much. Once again, she took charge and chose each of the nine courses with care.

Fifteen people gathered around the table that evening. I knew each one by name, and knew something about most of them. One worked at the post office, one had a father who was ninety-four, one repaired small machines, one was in university, one had a daughter living in Detroit, one was the family nuisance. But we were all together at that table, eating, talking and laughing. Michael took pictures of everyone in the room, in every possible combination. Afterwards, he hooked up his digital camera to the TV and showed the photographs he'd just taken. And we laughed some more.

Hours later, Michael and I sat in a taxi on our way back to the Ever Joint Hotel. The sky had turned dark as we drove along the river. I gazed out the window at the shiny black, watery surface shimmering in the moonlight. Our banquet had been a resounding success. Everyone would have left with a good memory. It had been a year since my first trip back to China, and in that year I had learned so much about the land of my birth and my family. Nevertheless, none of them knew the truth about my father. Several times I'd felt ready to tell my sister; she had a right to know. But each time something would constrict my throat, and my secret would stay inside me. What was the point? I asked myself. What was the point of destroying the image she held of her father as a powerful, confident man? In the depths of my soul, though, I knew that I was rationalizing my lack of courage. As hard as I tried, I could not rid myself of the shame that lurked inside me. I could not bring myself to utter the truth.

We were about to cross over the bridge that connected the city with the island where the hotel was located. Michael was speaking to me, but I had been lost in my thoughts. "That was some dinner we had," he repeated. "What do you think your father would have said if he could have seen you tonight?"

"He . . . ." The question did not surprise me, yet I hesitated, not knowing how to respond. For some unknown reason on that particular night, my husband's innocent comment stirred up the grief and anger I'd so long ago buried, settled and smoothed over, roused it like silt from the bottom of a riverbed. Those emotions swirled and seeped, unbidden, into every molecule of my being.

When I was a child, my father used to invoke an old Chinese proverb. *The first generation plants the tree; the next generation enjoys the shade.* By the time I was a teenager, this little homily had been repeated so often that I simply dismissed it. *Yeah. Yeah. I know . . . the next generation . . . .* I was sick of being reminded of my good fortune and the terrible deprivations my parents had survived. I could only think about myself, how I could hardly wait to strike out on my own. But now.

I pressed my forehead against the glass and peered into the darkness. The moon was smaller than it had been a few nights ago, when I'd seen it at the orange grove. My body felt limp; I bit my lip and willed myself to speak clearly. "He would have wept," I finally whispered. "He would have wept." Michael reached over and held my hand.

What would my father have said? Would he have said that his *gow meng,* his dog life, was finally worth it? Would his tears at least have been tears of joy?

I was sitting next to First Brother's widow in Lew's apartment. Again, I watched Jeen roll the round table out to the centre of the living room. Michael was on the balcony with Bing, looking at Wei's potted plants.

Later in the afternoon, we would leave for Shanghai, Suzhou, Hangzhou and Nanjing before returning home to Canada. Jeen had insisted that we have a final lunch with her, Bing, Lew, Wei, and First Brother's widow.

For our last meal together, my nephew had gone to even greater expense than usual: a plate of shrimp, a whole fish, vegetables stir-fried with black truffles, roasted duck. Jeen brought over a large bowl of steaming soup and set it down in the middle of the table. Wei started to ladle the broth into individual bowls. Lew was not only First Brother's son, he was also the spirit son of the brother "who lived above my head." He was my blood nephew and my spirit nephew, honouring the return of his aunt to the land of her birth.

I wondered when I might return to China. I thought of those green hills behind my father's village and how the sun sparkled off them on the day we'd visited, how they beckoned me to walk up the gentle slope. Sitting at the table and seeing my relatives around me, I knew that my next trip would be soon.

Then Jeen spoke, as if she had read my mind. "The next time you come back," she said, "I will pick an auspicious date and we will visit the graves. You can make an offering to First Mother." I agreed.

She then told me that after my mother's death, everyone in my family in China dressed in white mourning clothes and went back to Ning Kai Lee. They returned to the ancestral home and made an offering of cooked meat, sweet biscuits, tea and fruit in front of the shrine. They burned spirit money to bribe the evil spirits in the afterlife so my parents would have safe passage. Each person lit candles and sticks of incense, bowed three times and prayed to the ancestors, requesting their protection and blessing. Afterwards, they walked to the stream that flowed beside the village, and there they performed another ceremony and sang song after song, calling and calling the spirits of my father and my mother, over lakes, Prairies and mountains, across the deep Pacific, all the way back to their home. *Yes.* Their spirits were here in China where they belonged, a place where they might grasp the happiness that had eluded them in life.

I dipped my spoon into my bowl of hot soup. The broth was delicious, the goodness warming my heart.

ACKNOWLEDGEMENTS

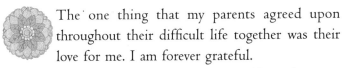The one thing that my parents agreed upon throughout their difficult life together was their love for me. I am forever grateful.

This memoir would not have been possible without my family in China and Canada sharing their stories and memories. I thank them for their generosity.

I give special thanks to my publisher, Anne Collins, for her steadfast support; to my editor, Craig Pyette, for always knowing the right questions to ask; to my agent, Denise Bukowski, for championing this project with such enthusiasm; to my copy editor, Kathryn Dean, for her keen and exacting eye; to Terri Nimmo for her spectacular and sensitive book design. Thanks to Shyam Selvadurai and Wayson Choy for reading early drafts and steering the manuscript in the right direction. To Larry Wong for helping me negotiate the archives at the Vancouver Public Library. To my niece Linda Fong for insights into the manuscript. To my dear friend Patricia O'Sullivan, for discussions and memories. And last but not least to Michael Bates for his hard work, patience, love and abiding faith.

I wish to acknowledge *The Rape of Nanking* by Iris Chang which gave me a sense of pre-war life in that city. I also wish to acknowledge the staff at the Vancouver Public Library who helped me locate information regarding pre WWI Chinese immigrants in Canada.

Thank you to the Toronto Arts Council, the Ontario Arts Council and the Canada Council whose financial assistance has helped in the realization of this work.